KING ALF

Family Support

Ruth Gardner

© Ruth Gardner 1998

Published by
VENTURE PRESS
16 Kent Street
Birmingham
B5 6RD

British Library Cataloguing-in-Publication Data
A catalogue record for this book is available from the
British Library

ISBN 1 86178 026 5 (paperback)

Design, layout and production by
Hucksters Advertising & Publishing Consultants,
Riseden, Tidebrook, Wadhurst, East Sussex TN5 6PA

Cover design by:
Western Arts
194 Goswell Road
London
EC1V 7DT

Printed and bound in Great Britain by
Biddles Ltd, Guildford and King's Lynn

Contents

Acknowledgements

For her support with this and and other projects, Silvana Marsh.

Members of the Communities and Colleagues in Hackney particularly:

> The Family Support Steering Group and NSPCC F.S. Development Team;
> The Area Child Protection Team;
> Homestart;
> NCH (Action for Children);
> Newpin.

Divisional Management Team, The Children's Society Senior Management and Children and Families Management Team, London Borough of Hackney

For other quotations:

> Peter Marsh and Gill Crow;
> Gerrilyn Smith;
> Jane Aldgate and Jane Tunstill;
> Pam Craig;
> Pauline Hardiker.

Defining terms

Different people often assume that they mean the same thing when they talk about family support, because these are 'motherhood and apple pie' terms – no one can disagree either with families or with supporting them.
Nevertheless 'family support' can mean very different things, depending on where the service is focused – the child, the child with parent(s) or the whole family within a particular community – and depending on the value base of the observer. Family support can mean **self-help** or volunteer help for family members with minimal outside involvement until the family itself identifies the need. It can mean a **continuum** of advice, support, and specialist help starting in the community and signposting families towards early, less traumatic intervention to avoid a crisis. And it can mean a specific approach, that is a way of dealing with life crises and problems, including abuse within families, which takes account of any strengths and positive relationships within these same families which could assist recovery.

In the Children Act 1989 family support is broadly defined as a local authority (not just a social services) duty. The broader local authority or corporate responsibility is very significant. Recent reorganisation has often resulted in combined housing and social services, or education and social services departments. Even where this is not the case, separate departments have often combined ideas and resources to address particular needs – for instance the housing and support needs of young people leaving care or the developmental and care needs of pre-school children.

The corporate duty as set out in the Act is:

> (a) to safeguard and promote the welfare of children within their area who are in need; and
>
> (b) so far as is consistent with that duty, to promote the upbringing of such children by their families by providing a range and level of services appropriate to those children's needs.
>
> ***Children Act 1989 S.17***

This legal definition of support demands a focus both on the individual child and on the birth family as the preferred (but not the only possible) context for child development. Schedule 2 of the Act sets out a range of services of which day care and family centres are two required elements, and thus the legislation links the family of the child in need to community-based provision. The definition of a child in need, here, is all important and relates clearly to individual developmental criteria. Not only does the local authority need to collaborate well internally to meet these needs but external collaborations, particularly with health purchasers and providers, are also essential. The term 'collaborative advantage' is used to describe the pay-off for working well together, as opposed to the more familiar term 'competitive advantage'.

> *...a child shall be taken to be in need if*
> *(a) he is unlikely to achieve or maintain, or to have the*
> *opportunity of achieving or maintaining, a reasonable*
> *standard of health or development without the provision*
> *for him of services by a local authority under this Part;*
> *(b) his health or development is likely to be significantly*
> *impaired, or further impaired, without the provision for*
> *him of such services; or*
> *(c) he is disabled,*
> *and "family", in relation to such a child, includes any*
> *person who has parental responsibility for the child and*
> *any other person with whom he has been living.*
> **Children Act 1989 S.17**

Various less formal and legalistic definitions of family support have been put forward. The following attempts to capture the purpose and nature (the why and how) of family support were endorsed by voluntary and statutory agencies attempting to achieve a joint strategy for family support in an inner London borough:

> *"Advice and assistance from informal or formal sources*
> *which help families to bring up children and young*
> *people at home. Formal interventions are minimised,*
> *and where necessary are introduced in a timely, sensitive*
> *way with as little damage to the family as possible."*
> **Gardner 1996**

While it still begs many questions, it avoids 'needs testing' of the individual child or family and affirms that the whole continuum of provision, from voluntary visiting to care proceedings and beyond, can be turned towards strengthening the family rather than undermining it.

Yet another definition avoids seeing family support as a 'propping-up exercise' to the family – one of the aspects of the term 'support' which some families dislike. Instead the context is emphasised as highly influential on the type of action taken. We know, for instance, that families often find it difficult to approach social services before a crisis, but that the same workers in a non-social services setting are seen as less intimidating...

> *"a climate or setting in which individuals or groups can take positive action on their own behalf – empowerment"*.
>
> **Warren 1997**

Family support provision, Warren argues, needs to combine both one-to-one counselling skills and more collective practice associated with community development. Warren states that to empower families to act on their own behalf requires a range of skills from practitioners. He sees social workers and community workers as having a very different agenda when they undertake group work. The social work agenda is usually 'emotional support and the group's capacity to nurture and strengthen members', and those of community work are more often directed to external goals and valuing 'leadership and a range of technical skills and knowledge' in the group that will attain those goals. If individual practitioners cannot achieve this continuum, he asks, could training help, or does it require yet another set of skills to manage or deploy a range of practitioners? Such a broad definition of support has to be analysed in this way to assist understanding.

If you are developing your policy or practice in relation to family support, you must take time out to discuss and reach some clarity about definitions. This will almost inevitably lead to a debate about values and principles, with possibly very divergent perspectives. The debate may be frustrating for some but it is essential, in order discover any common ground. The formats set out below and on page 62 may help you to hold this discussion.

Clarifying our Intentions

Purpose (Mission)

Why are we setting out to achieve a Family Support Strategy/Policy/Service Development/Project? What are the motivators (Values/Demand/Legal/ Budgetary)? Who is committed?

End Result (Vision)

What is it we want to achieve – if we had a Family Support Strategy/Policy/ Service Development/Project, what would it look like and what would be the concrete benefits? You may want to brainstorm to collect many ideas but in the end you should be as specific and concrete as possible i.e. "A document signed by three agencies, health, education, and social services"; "an advice service on a 24-hour basis" etc. This is where you will need to have clear, agreed definitions of any terms you use. Who is still committed?

Risk Assessment

What risks and difficulties must be addressed, e.g. how do we ensure children's views are heard? That the work is safe for children?

Success Criteria

How will we know that we have achieved the end result? What are the **essential** features of, or prerequisites to, success? How will we **measure** achievement? In numbers and/or user views for example?

Information

What information/data, resources, and skills do we already have that are relevant to achieving the End Result? What are the gaps? Do they jeopardise the End Result?

What Has To Be Done

What are the main sub-tasks needed? If necessary, break the process down into phases and complete a plan for each phase, with targets. Who is still committed?

Plan

Who will be responsible for each sub-task and in what timescale? You may want to use project management techniques to break the process down yet further and cost each activity. Who is still committed?

This format is provided by Coverdale Consultancy (with modifications)

Child protection practice is not immune from the debate about definitions or boundaries. In most cases the Children Act definitions of 'harm' are used, which (as with 'need') very much centre on the individual child.

> *"Ill-treatment or the impairment of health or development"*
> *"development" means physical, intellectual, social or behavioural development*
> *"health" means physical or mental health*
> *"ill-treatment" includes sexual abuse and forms of ill-treatment which are not physical*
>
> **Children Act 1989 S.31**

Definitions of harm in child protection procedures emphasise categories or types of incident which lead to registration of a child as 'at risk':

> **Neglect:** *The persistent or severe neglect of the child, or failure to protect a child from exposure to any kind of danger including cold and starvation, or extreme failure to carry out important aspects of care, resulting in the significant impairment of the child's health and development, including non-organic failure to thrive.*
> **Physical abuse:** *Actual or likely physical injury to a child, or failure to prevent physical injury (or suffering) to a child, including deliberate poisoning, suffocation, and Munchausen's Syndrome by proxy.*
>
> **Working Together under the Children Act 1989 HMSO**

Recent research shows that the context of family life (the 'climate') can be oppressive and/or cold and rejecting, and at least as harmful to a child as any particular incident.

> *It has been demonstrated that any potentially abusive incident has to be seen in context before the extent of its harm can be assessed and appropriate interventions effected. Many of the studies show that, with the exception of a few severe assaults and some sexual maltreatment, long-term difficulties for children seldom follow from a single abusive event; rather they are more likely to be the consequence of living in an unfavourable environment, particularly one which is low in warmth and high in criticism.*
>
> **Messages from Research HMSO 1997**

Gerrilyn Smith argues that all non-abusing adults in a community have a responsibility to children:

"Surrounding any child in the community is a network of adults. Within this network are both possible protectors and perpetrators, with the former outnumbering the latter. This book aims to transform non-abusing adults into protectors, by providing information regarding sexual abuse that will help to reduce the risk of its occurring and aid the recovery of those who have already experienced it."

Smith 1995, p.78

THE OFFENDER-ORGANISED SYSTEM: KEEPING IT CHILD-CENTRED

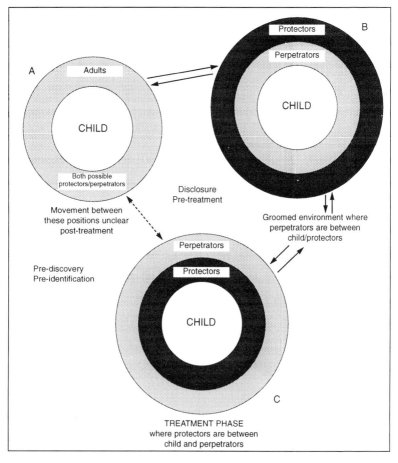

Others have put forward a much broader sociological definition of significant harm which includes collective and institutional responsibility for child welfare. This would then include communal and environmental sources of avoidable harm to children, such as traffic accidents, poor housing, and pollutants. These, arguably, are the cause of far more developmental damage to children than individual cases of abuse. But collective responsibility is harder to pin down and rarely the task of a single agency.

SUMMARY

In the area of child welfare, and particularly when new ideas are under debate, terms are not fixed and are used to convey different meanings depending on the context and the point of view of the person using them. It is therefore very important not simply to accept and use terms but to ask *"what do I/you/we mean by this?"* and if necessary write down any agreed definitions. They may change over time, but at least you know where you started. When the question *"what do I mean by family support?"* is asked, the answer often prompts more questions and this in turn can lead to creative dialogue and ideas. If these questions are avoided, people or groups who think they are working towards the same goal can be in for disappointment and confusion when they are some way down the line, and this can wreck joint planning.

Values and principles

The pressure to gear services towards prevention received a boost from the UN and European Conventions on the Rights of the Child. The UN Convention (adopted by the UN General Assembly in 1989 and by the UK government in 1991) sets out in 54 articles the responsibilities of parents and States for the welfare and normal development of children.

Examples are:

- Article 2 sets out the principle that all rights apply to all children without exception; and the State's obligation to protect children from any form of discrimination.
- Article 5 sets out the State's duty to respect the rights and responsibilities of parents and the wider family to provide appropriate direction and guidance to children.
- Articles 13 and 14 set out the child's right to freedom of expression, thought, conscience and religion, subject to appropriate particular guidance and national law.
- Article 18 sets out the principle that parents have joint responsibility for bringing up children and that States should give assistance to them and develop appropriate facilities including child care for working parents.
- Article 24 sets out the right to the highest attainable standards of health and access to services with special emphasis on primary and preventive health care and working towards the abolition of harmful traditional practices.

Newell 1991 Appendix 1

These principles clearly underpin the Children Act and the recognition that a wide range of agencies – health, education, housing, leisure, voluntary, cultural and religious groups – all have a contribution to child development in the broadest sense.

In terms of the debate outlined in the previous chapter, between protection and prevention, The Children Act 1989 also tried to balance two major elements in child care – the child's rights to protection and **wider family rights to**

remain a viable unit. The 1980s threw up a number of child care controversies over these issues. One example was Jasmine Beckford's death at the hands of her parents, considered to be partly the result of under reaction by social services (L.B. Brent 1985). Another was the Cleveland crisis, where the media stated that children were removed from families and family contact as the result of over-zealous and intrusive social work. A public inquiry was set up (HMSO 1988) which recognised that *"it is a delicate and difficult line to tread between taking action too soon and not taking it soon enough"*, and led to improved awareness of social workers' role as **representatives** of society's very ambiguous attitudes to children.

The outcome was

"a wish for legislation and policy to attempt to proceed in two directions at once – both toward better protection for the child and better protection of the parent".
The Children Act could either be seen as an
"attempt to avoid the awkward dilemmas that the child care field inevitably throws up" or *"a genuinely more effective balance, correcting tendencies both to over- and under-react, while helping parents and children as a unit where it is appropriate to do so".*

Fox Harding 1991

The Act itself sets out important criteria for decisions made in court, which require consideration of the child as a person, as well as her family and background. Also, the "non-interventionist" stance, taken from mental health legislation, challenges workers to consider the outcomes of their actions, and whether intervention is likely to be of benefit, in advance of making influential decisions .

Children Act 1989 Section I

S.1.3 In the circumstances mentioned in sub-section(4), a court shall have regard in particular to:

(a) the ascertainable wishes and feelings of the child concerned (considered in the light of his age and understanding);

(b) his physical, emotional and educational needs;

(c) the likely effect on him of any change in his circumstances;   ▶

◀
(d) his age, sex, background and any characteristics of his which the court considers relevant;

(e) any harm that he has suffered or is at risk of suffering;

(f) how capable each of his parents, and any other person in relation to whom the court considers the question to be relevant, is of meeting his needs;

(g) the range of powers available to the court under this Act in the proceedings in question.

S.1.5 Where a court is considering whether or not to make one or more orders under this Act with respect to a child, it shall not make the order or any of the orders unless it considers that doing so would be better for the child than making no order at all.

The Act also sets out broad parameters for family support services in Part III and Schedule 2 **before** going on to describe child protection duties and powers in Part IV. The definition of children in need encompasses those in need of protection so that, where protection is an issue, family support must also be considered. The alternative is to define children in need as only those who need protection. When some minimalist authorities attempted to do this, a DoH circular (17.1.91) pronounced that narrow definition of need to be over-restrictive and unlawful.

Principles and Practice for Guidance and Legislation *HMSO 1989* conveys some of the important themes underlying the Act, echoing the *UN Convention of the Rights of the Child.* These themes include:

1. The individuality of each child, which should be respected, including age, gender, health, personality, race, culture and life experience;

2. The universality of some needs, such as healthy development, protection from all forms of exploitation, education, etc. which all adults and agencies must provide;

3. The unique advantages for children in experiencing normal family life and the need to preserve the home and/or positive family links as far as possible, using a wide variety of services;

4. The needs of parents and carers should be considered as part of this aim;

5. The need for co-operation between individuals and agencies in order to achieve positive outcomes for children and families.

It is worth restating that no single agency or group has the resources or skills to provide family support on its own. The Children Act 1989 lays the duties in Part III on the **whole local authority**, not just one department; and requires joint provision and co-operation between agencies and departments.

S.17 (5) Every local authority:

(a) shall facilitate the provision by others including in particular voluntary organisations of services which the authority have power to provide by virtue of this section or Section 18, 20, 23, or 14 and

(b) may make such arrangements as they see fit for any person to act on their behalf in the provision of such a service.

Children Act 1989

We have focused on the Children Act 1989 because it challenges local authorities to consider the wider needs of families as the context for specific intervention to protect children. However, other legislation, for instance on health, housing, education and social security, is equally significant. The following table, drawn up by the Audit Commission, underlines the degree of co-operation needed if services are to be well targeted and co-ordinated.

The need for collaborative provision – identified by LAs	
1. Health	Respite care, disability register Services for Under 8s
2. Health/Education	Support service for children looked after Services for children with special needs Information for children with disabilities Treatment service for abused children Training for child protection
3. Health/Education/ Social Services	Joint register and joint commissioning for children with disabilities Joint commissioning therapeutic services Specialist disability teams for children Services for children out of school and for children with emotional difficulties ▶

◀

The need for collaborative provision – identified by LAs

4. Health/Voluntary Agencies	Respite/support care services
	After school services
	Counselling services for young people in distress
5. Local Education Departments	Education for young people looked after
	Positive response to truancy
	Educational achievement programme
	Early years services
	Provision for EDB children
	Provision for children excluded from school
	Provision for reducing numbers of children out of school
	Education for special needs children
	Day EDB provision and support unit
6. Housing	Housing provision for young people who leave care or who are homeless
	After carer
	Support accommodation
	Shared housing schemes
	Services for 16 plus
	Housing and advice
	Housing for vulnerable young people
	Housing for young people leaving care
7. Probation Service	Community action diversion from crime programme
	Youth Justice Service
8. Probation/Housing/ Education and Police	Community action diversion from crime programme
	Youth Justice Service
	Day care services for children in need
	Early years curriculum with education
	Homelessness for 16- and 17-year-olds
9. Voluntary sector	Day care services for children in need
	Early years curriculum with education
	Homelessness for 16- and 17-year-olds

Source: Seen but not Heard 1994 HMSO

The "welfare to work" and social exclusion agendas, set
out by the Labour administration of 1997, aim to bring
together public and private resources to tackle the related
issues of poverty, unemployment, lone parenthood, and
the need for good quality child care in ways that require
massive co-ordination. Early years development plans,
usually drawn up within local authority education
departments, can now draw on social services, health, and
voluntary sector skills in order to provide the widest
possible range of assistance to parents and young children.

SUMMARY

The development of family support theory and practice
rests on a number of wider societal and legal changes.
The recognition of children's rights both internationally
and nationally is one such change. Children's rights
include both the right to protection and the right to live,
wherever possible, within their birth family with support
that prevents them coming to harm. There has also been a
shift in perspective concerning children and families in
difficulty; rather than setting the child versus the parent or
the family versus the State, there is a greater willingness to
see most family difficulties as normal, requiring
recognition of mutual responsibilities and a number of
different strands of protection and support. Amid
continuing controversy about the threshold for State
intervention on behalf of the child, and when family
difficulties should become a public concern, there is also
greater appreciation that social workers and others make a
judgement on behalf of the community. This threshold is
to some extent everyone's responsibility and shifts
according to knowledge, values, and beliefs. Individuals
who pose a persistent and irremediable threat to children,
whether from within or outside the family, are hard to
identify and prosecute even for those with extensive
experience. It is just as hard to address those
circumstances and settings which are inherently damaging
to children's potential and these issues are now
demanding joint effort across professional boundaries, as
well as being raised to the national political agenda.

Quality and equality

What is 'good' family support? Clearly this depends upon our definition, which in turn depends on basic values and principles. Some of these values, such as respect for the individual, are held in common across the whole range of adult interaction with children from home to school, to hospital or residential care. Quality is now a popular subject for a number of reasons. Quality-management systems have arisen in the manufacturing industry where quality means *"complete conformance to customer requirements"* – that the product unfailingly does what the customer needs or wants it to do.

Quality assurance in the purest sense includes providing a **formal, recognised quality management system** which guarantees product conformance, together with periodic audit of that system's effectiveness, and **review and revision of the system** to meet changing requirements.

Total Quality Management (TQM) applies these three principles to every worker and each process within an organisation, from office cleaning to letter-writing.

> *Everyone, starting with management, is encouraged to refuse to accept the inevitability of errors and to concentrate on preventing errors occurring in the first place. To achieve this, individuals must be provided with the skills, tools, and authority to investigate problems and introduce improvements.*

These systems do not only apply to 'hard' requirements such as delivery times or product reliability; they also apply to 'soft' requirements, relating to customer perception of the product or service, and the authors say of these less-direct elements of a service that:

> *These factors convey a message to customers about whether they are welcome, or just a nuisance. Are they kept waiting? This indicates to a customer that you believe your time is more valuable than theirs; it is not.*
> **Munroe-Faure and Munroe-Faure 1994**

They include such matters as telephone answering and correspondence, accessibility, maintenance and security of buildings; hospitality and the manner in which meetings are conducted; courtesy and promptness.

It is in these areas that public services have tended to fail. The Chartermark initiatives have set standards for improvement in service delivery, and Investors In People (IIP) sets standards for staff training and development.

Often with the best of intentions, social services have given very negative and unsupportive messages to children, young people, and families. For instance it is often the case that:

- in order not to 'waste public money', reception areas are poorly lit and decorated, infrequently cleaned and uncomfortable; there is no safe area for small children;
- visitors to reception are not filtered by the type of assistance sought, and clear notices about the service are not displayed so that many wait, only to be turned away;
- appointments systems are not used or not maintained;
- keeping the office open at all times is considered more important than ensuring that the minimum paperwork and follow-up requirements are met to guarantee results. This is often a political requirement because office hours are so visible. It means workers are always playing 'catch-up' on arrears of administrative and paperwork, and responses are delayed;
- because of pressure of other work, meetings are held without preparation, the necessary documents, or even the key people present. As a result, families end up confused and angry, and a support approach is jeopardised from the start.

If any of these scenarios ring true (and not only for social services!), quality systems are worth considering. **Process analysis** means looking at an activity in detail from beginning to end and considering each "transaction" within that process, for instance **a health visitor meeting with a mother to draw up a plan for health checks**. The mother is the ultimate user or customer and her views on the service a major element in its evaluation. At an earlier stage, though, if a typist is to produce the plan legibly to deadline she is a supplier and the health visitor is a customer for that part of the process. If the plan is to be delivered to social services in time for a needs assessment conference, the health visitor is supplier and the social worker the customer. If the parent has agreed to undertake a task, he or she is also responsible for coming up with the goods. At each state the **user/customer requirements** need to be clear, the **possible failures identified**, and the **process requirements** to eliminate them supplied. In the case of the health visitors plan the analysis might be:

Customer for the written plan:	social worker
Provider:	health visitor
Possible failures:	1. Delayed/no meeting with mother
	2. Plan not forthcoming
	3. Not enough time to write
	4. No typing
Requirements:	1. Set date for meeting well in advance, or meet at health centre
	2. Send outline plan/ideas for comment to mother
	3. Set aside two hours for write up
	4. Ask X to type ten days before conference and fax to SW.
	5. Check at each stage.

The advantage of these approaches is that they start with the user of the service at each stage, and her or his total requirements. It is not good enough to have an advice and information service which is second to none if the building it is housed in is miles from a bus route, or a child protection service which is sound but offers no translation service for half its potential users. This approach means that each individual takes responsibility, **and credit**, for achieving tasks that contribute to the final outcome.

The Social Services Inspectorate has developed 25 standards with associated criteria for the inspection of family support services for children in need. They address these questions:

> *Is this agency complying with legal requirements?*
> *What are service users receiving from this agency?*
> *How are equal opportunities incorporated into the services?*

Some of the standards are about process, e.g.

> *a recorded plan is constructed with the involvement of the child, the child's parents, other family members and carers, and relevant agencies.*

Others are about overall strategy in service provision,

> *the local authority co-ordinates work with other agencies*

and yet others are about quality control within the agency:

> *The SSD has identified the knowledge and skills required for providing services for children in need and their families and has a clear management plan for the training and development of all staff.*
>
> **SSI 1996**

Such standards include 'hard' requirements such as a plan written presumably within a time frame, and 'job requirements' such as 'taking into account wishes and feelings of the child' which may entail a different kind of measurement, perhaps ensuring that the child's views are recorded at every review and their wishes followed up.

It is less easy to set standards where the work is taking place in the community. Some broad but defining principles and standards have been developed based on work in the US, for instance Warren 1997:

1. Does the policy or practice enhance a sense of community among its members?
2. Does the policy or practice promote the flow of resources and supports to and from the family?
3. Does the policy or practice encourage shared responsibility and collaboration between the family and professional service providers?
4. Does the policy or practice strengthen and protect the integrity of the family unit?
5. Does the policy or practice operate to enhance and promote the competence of the family and individual family members?
6. Does the policy or practice encourage service delivery approaches that are consistent with the above principles?

Warren 1997

Each of these principles or standards has been detailed
further with a set of criteria, for instance question 2 above
is broken down to include:

> *2.4 Does the policy/practice encourage a balance
> between the use of informal and formal sources of
> support?*

and 4. includes:

> *4.4 Does the policy/practice prevent the possibility of
> abuse or neglect, by enhancing the flow of resources and
> promoting behaviour incompatible with maltreatment?*

These standards at a first reading may seem difficult to
measure but clearly it is possible to build a profile of the
different kinds of family support being provided and, for
instance, to show how community groups promote child
safety – by organising safe play areas, checking volunteers,
and helping parents and children in awareness of potential
abuse and confidence in challenging abusers. The
assessor is asked to judge whether the evidence that the
standard is being met is strong, questionable or weak, and
to give examples.

The difference between standards and criteria,
performance measures or indicators is that, while
standards can be general and aspirational, measures or
indicators are concrete, specific, and observable. One
major problem with a lot of family support work is that
evidence about the work is neither sought nor kept. The
SSI asked eight social services departments for file records
on a range of cases but "none were able to respond
satisfactorily because they did not routinely keep
information about referrals". This is just as true of
voluntary organisations, large and small.

There may be good reasons why this is so – the cost of
record keeping, client confidentiality, informality – but
without any account of a service, however anonymised and
summarised, that service is invisible and highly vulnerable.
Users of a service often help to build up a record of the
work if they accept its value and such a history adds value
to what has been achieved.

Evaluation and monitoring are more familiar terms for the process of quality control, and pose the same challenges. The group or organisation, however small, has, for instance, to decide:

- what are we trying to achieve? for whom? (outcomes);
- have we asked users what they want? (consultation);
- how do we deliver what is needed? (process, activities);
- what resources does this require? (time, skills, equipment, etc – inputs);
- what are the costs?;
- are we achieving our agreed objectives? (outputs);
- how can we measure our achievement (indicators of performance).

Monitoring can be both **quantitative**, in terms of hours of provision offered, numbers of families taking part in a certain range of activities, etc., and **qualitative**, seeking user or/and referrer views in a structured way. But it must be regular and consistent, i.e. comparing the same elements over time, or at least indicating clearly what changes have occurred.

Evaluation involves a fuller assessment of monitoring and other data (e.g. annual reports, complaints, accounts) in order to assess a group's or organisation's achievements in relation to its resources, and possibly to compare it with other activities with similar aims. As with planning (see chapter on *Planning for results*) if groups do not set their own criteria and monitor their own work, preferably using an independent observer, they are increasingly likely to find funders doing this instead. Independent evaluation need not be expensive or undermining; local further or higher educational establishments will often provide a small-scale evaluation which can be confidential to the organisation if it so wishes. Well-organised monitoring can be a source of real learning and benefit, demonstrating that user requirements are being addressed and giving providers valuable data to improve the service. (See Adirondack 1989.)

If the organisation or group is not achieving any benefits, or there is dissatisfaction with the service the sooner this can be tackled by those actively involved the better.

EQUALITY

Equality has rightly been set alongside quality as an integral but particularly significant element of best practice. Often it is innovative work with children and families in "minority" groups which sets a trend and informs mainstream services; for example, respite care for families with children infected or affected by HIV/AIDS (Barnardos) work with travelling communities (Save the Children). Both statutory and voluntary sectors have contributed to this new work. In this book we have referred to such work within the text; see particularly chapter on *Planning for results*, where the examples include issues of identity, culture, and ethnicity as the Children Act demands; and *Activities – practical illustrations* chapter, where examples are given of successful activities particularly designed by and for parents and children from ethnic minorities. As more such activities are evaluated, so family support that builds on the strengths of minority groups (rather than seeing them as 'problems') will develop its own knowledge base, standards, and goals.

The Children's Society, a national charity, used a cross-section of its staff working in a variety of projects across the country to develop **anti-discrimination practice standards** for service users (see below). These can be monitored by the projects and by users to develop better awareness and a fairer, more open service.

OVERALL STANDARD

In all our work with children, young people, and adults we shall:
- Respect diversity;
- Use language that is understandable and respectful;
- Plan for environmental features which are sensitive to difference;
- Create and offer opportunities for individuals and groups to express their views and be heard;
- Work in a way that aims to ensure they have opportunities and choice as well as responsibilities towards others;
- Think about the existence of, and potential for, oppressive experiences and practice of both those with whom we work and staff.

Standard 1

Initial information to potential users is welcoming, easy to understand, accurate, and up to date, containing sufficient information to enable the person to make a choice about their use of the service.

Standard 2

Children, young people, and adults using the service are welcomed, responded to as individuals, and provided with the information they need.

Standard 3

The environment, whether it is a building, an office, or one without a building base, enables children, young people, and adults to feel safe, comfortable and respected.

Standard 4

Divisional and project systems, policies, and everyday practices should all respect the different needs of children, young people, and adults.

Standard 5

Children, young people, and adults are able to raise concerns, make complaints easily and know that they will be responded to promptly, positively and fairly through the use of the agreed procedures.

Standard 6

Challenge all language, behaviour, processes, etc. which oppress children, young people, and adults within the Children's Society or in our working relations with external individuals or organisations.

Standard 7

The Standards and their implementation will be monitored and reviewed on a regular basis within projects and the Division, in order to monitor progress, identify areas for change and as a contribution to the further development of the Standards. This process must involve children, young people, and adults, as well as staff.

Standard 8

The anti-discrimination standards are implemented and become a fundamental and active part of practice in the Division, providing the framework for exploration, development, and action.

The Children's Society Anti-Discrimination Practice
Standards Work in Progress October 1996

SUMMARY

Quality is a fashionable word but should not be avoided – the process of defining and testing quality in family support, though at the exploratory stage, is extremely important. This is, firstly, because we must overcome the perception of work with families and children that is less formal and imposed as somehow an 'add on' which may be well intentioned but is poorly structured and possibly wasteful. More importantly, many projects do make an enormous difference according to families themselves and we need evidence of this 'difference' or impact in order to build on what works. This is particularly true of work with groups traditionally marginalised or defined as 'problematic'; families where there is a member with a disability; and ethnic minorities, for instance. Increasingly, specific groups are developing their own innovative services. Three main types of quality control are outlined above. First, process analysis to ensure that key tasks are broken down and each part is completed satisfactorily. Second, setting broad standards and breaking these down into criteria with indicators or measurements for which there is evidence, such as a child's developmental progress or parent's contacts in the community. Third, evaluation and monitoring of specific projects to check that they are meeting agreed goals, including most importantly the goals of the people on the receiving end.

Relevant theory and research findings

The theory of prevention has provided the basis for the theory of family support. There have been numerous discussions of the difficulties involved in applying preventive theory to research, much less practice (see Hardiker *et al.* 1991).

It is very hard to establish links between cause and effect that are strong enough to prove that any particular activity is preventive of a social problem. In some cases there are reasonably clear links, e.g. between drink-driving campaigns and a reduction in related accidents; more often a number of other 'preventive' causes can be established.

The term 'prevention' can be used to apply to work with individuals and also with groups or whole populations. It can be used at different stages of a problem's development.

> *Primary prevention is thought of as comprising those services which provide support to families and reduce the general levels of poverty, stress, insecurity, ill health and bad housing... "Secondary" prevention is more specific. Once problems have actually arisen, help of various kinds may supply a remedy or at least forestall something worse. At this stage, services are liable to be restricted to those who are assumed to be at "special risk" or whose circumstances warrant special priority.*
>
> ***Parker 1980***

Pauline Hardiker and her colleagues at Leicester University have refined this theory to include, alongside those 'stages' of preventive activity, the type of welfare policy being applied by the agency. In their view, these 'models of welfare' – residual, institutional, and developmental – underpin provision as follows:

In a residual model, the care of children is not seen to be the proper business of the state; emphasis is placed on individual freedoms and parental rights and duties. Social work is largely about social control in this model. With an institutional model, the state is given a greater role in tempering the consequences of individualism and the free market, such as ill-health, unemployment and poverty. The normality of difficulties in rearing children in a complex and changing society is recognised. Professional social workers assess needs and may provide a wide range of services to address them. This could be seen as a more humane form of social control...which aims to help reintegrate children and families into society rather than to rescue children and punish parents. Developmental models give the state an even greater role in promoting conditions for a more just and equal society: social services adopt a promotional role for all citizens and aim to reduce social disadvantage. Empowerment, mediation, advocacy and community participation are the preferred methods. There are elements of all three models in contemporary childcare.

Hardiker et al. 1991

Hardiker's model is often shown as a matrix or grid combining three or four levels of prevention with three different types of welfare model described above. As a result it becomes possible to 'map' the type and amount of preventive and support services being provided in a particular area. On the following pages the grid is shown, then a set of services mapped onto it. This exercise encourages debate and highlights gaps. For instance, local authorities may be providing a 'last resort', highly reactive service to asylum seekers in the form of food vouchers where preventive health and employment advice is necessary.

THE SOCIAL POLICY CONTEXTS OF CHILD WELFARE

THE ENABLING AUTHORITY

Level of Intervention	Welfare Model Role of the State		
	Last Resort	Needs Based	Combating Social Disadvantages
FIRST Populations: Diversion			Community Development
SECOND Early Risks		Counselling and Social Care Planning	
THIRD Serious Risks	Remedial Interventions		
FOURTH Rehabilitation	Planning for Permanence. Damage Limitation		

Hardiker et al: University of Leicester

PREVENTIVE & SUPPORT SERVICES – EXAMPLES

	Last Resort	Needs Based	Combating Social Disadvantages
First Level Diversion (large populations of groups)	1. Travellers Sites and support	1. Health Advice and Advocacy in communities. 2. Benefits Advice. 3. Advice Centre for Young People. 4. Parents' Centre. 5. Asian Women's Advice . 6. Turkish Advice Centre.	1. Income/debt. 2 Free healthcare. 3. Housing. 4. Crime prevention. 5. Parenting advice.
Second Level Early Risks ('In Need' S.17)	1. Asylum seekers advice routes	1. Community Psychologists', support to Health Visitors groups. 2. CFCS support to schools. 3. Diagnosis and support for children with disabilities. 4. Needs assessment. 5. Developing flexible care. 6. Homestart. 7. Newpin.	1. Youth work on estates.
Third: Serious Risks ('Significant Harm S.47)	1. Emergency and Police Protection Orders	1. CP Investigations. 2. Domestic Violence Refuge. 3. Substance Misuse. 4. S.20 Accommodation.	1. PR campaign to support parenting 2 YP leaving care *Support *Education *Housing
Fourth: Follow-up and LT Support		1. CFCS Therapy/ Treatment. 2 Long Term Respite and Flexible Care (e.g. HIV/ AIDS). 3. Adoption – and Post-adoption. 4. Work with Young Abusers.	

Gardner 1996 using Leicester grid

Research into family support and prevention also throws up many difficulties. The activities under scrutiny are often ill-defined and/or changing; measures of "success" may well be different for the child, the parent(s) and the referring agency; and outcomes such as improved well-being or social interaction may be attributable to causes other than the activity under research. Large-scale, longitudinal studies with control groups are the most informative, but they are costly, and the politicians and administrators who pay for research want quick results. In some cases it may also be considered unethical to assign children to a control group which will not receive a particular service.

The High Scope, pre-School education programme in the US is one of the best-known provisions evaluated over two decades.

Evaluating the effectiveness of High/Scope

High/Scope is one of the few curricula to have been evaluated on a long term basis. The High/Scope Perry Pre-school Project study focuses on the lives of 123 young people born between 1958 and 1962. The study began in 1962 with the selection of a group of three- and four-year-olds and continued over the following three years by the annual selection of additional groups of three-year-olds. The families were poor; 50 per cent were on welfare and 47 per cent had absent fathers. Study subjects were randomly assigned to a group that did go to pre-school or to a group that did not.

The programme was designed to assist children in combating the negative scholastic effects of poverty, an idea generally embodied in the Head Start programme. Head Start is a compensatory governmentally initiated educational programme in the USA, set up in the 1960s in response to the high levels of academic failure experienced throughout and beyond formal schooling particularly in low- and moderate-income families. Head Start encompasses a variety of initiatives including High/Scope. The High/Scope curriculum was one of the first to be incorporated into an experimental design that permitted researchers to trace its effects throughout the subsequent lives of participants. The findings of this longitudinal study indicated that the pre-school programme had a variety of short and long term benefits for children, when compared with children who did not attend any pre-school programme. These differences were most striking in the areas of achievement, motivation and social behaviour.

At age 19 High/Scope participants were found to have experienced less failure throughout schooling: for example 67 per cent of the High/Scope group graduated from high school as opposed to 49 per cent of the no pre-school group: they had a lower arrest rate; a lower teenage pregnancy rate; and higher employment and participation in further education.

Similarly at age 27, High/Scope participants were found to be more socially responsible. For example only one-fifth as many programme group members as no-programme group members were arrested five or more times; they were economically better off (for example, more likely to be home-owners and to own second cars); and more likely to have experienced educational success (for example one-third as many no-programme group members as programme group members graduated from regular or adult high school).

National Children's Bureau Highlight 1995

Evaluation of many such programmes indicated that while some short term effects such as higher IQ levelled out after a few years, longer term effects, such as improved employment chances and educational attainment of the next generation, were significant.

Many of the principles of Headstart programmes have been incorporated, or developed further, within pre-school and primary education in the UK, as a result of these long term findings, and Barnardos has provided training and support for Headstart initiatives. At the time of writing, longitudinal studies of similar programmes are being set up for the first time in the UK, and interest in this work is heightened.

In the US there has been a far greater commitment to evaluating family support programmes and drawing together the findings, giving useful practical indications for planners (see also the later chapter on *Planning for results*). One such overview compares the benefits of targeted as against universally accessible programmes and suggests among other features of successful family support, that a clear action plan and an active leader or "policy entrepreneur" are more important than the nature of the agency (health, education, etc.) hosting the project. It indicates that financing needs to be flexible, drawing on a number of sources, and that cost:benefit analysis should provide an assessment of benefits across department and agencies – for example, a programme identifying and supporting absentees from school may avoid later juvenile justice expenditure and lead the relevant agencies to support further joint ventures, which will shunt costs but also benefits back and forth over a number of projects (Marsh and Cramer 1992).

In the UK there have been significantly fewer such studies. The DoH-funded *Studies in Local Areas* (Gibbons 1990) looked at voluntary and statutory provision prior to the Children Act 1989.

The findings indicate, perhaps unsurprisingly, that where there are multiple sources of support (including family, friends, volunteers, and, most significantly, day care) parents under stress more easily overcame their problems.

However, the family support projects were struggling
with a number of issues:

- short term or single issue financing;
- tension between service provision (e.g. day care,
  assessment), and wider community development or advocacy
  needs, support to specific families under stress;
- tension between equal access aspirations, and actual use –
  which tended to be by white women and children, with very
  little use by local ethnic minority residents or by men;
- lack of infrastructure for project managers or their
  committees, e.g. administration, training, accountancy,
  personnel, policies such as child protection, etc.

Gibbons 1990

Social services, on the other hand, were:

- working with more lone parents and more materially
  disadvantaged parents;
- most commonly dealing with financial problems of people
  turned away by social security.

Gibbons 1990

The researcher felt that, for these users, trained volunteers
backed by welfare rights and legal specialists offered a
much more appropriate service than that of social workers,
who might then be free to offer better quality assessment
and support to families with complex difficulties.

Such findings were greatly enlarged and reinforced by
the distillation of 17 individual studies on child protection
work in the late 80s and early 90s. (Messages from
Research, 1995.) Most of the child care practice under
scrutiny either took place before the Children Act or in the
transitional period, so may have been refined since.
However, the overarching messages are that too much
emphasis is placed on investigating specific abusive
incidents rather than making enquiries about, and
assessing needs in, the whole family.

In a study published in 1991, the author found that the
majority of parents (including fathers) had serious physical

and/or mental health problems which had only rarely been known to social workers concerned about standards of child care (Gardner 1991). More recently, guidance on parents who use drugs states that unless there are specific risks of significant harm to children, family support services meeting the assessed needs of both parent and child are the preferred option (Local Government Association 1997).

As we have indicated, large scale research suggests that single abusive incidents are unlikely, except in extreme cases, to lead to long term difficulties for children – a home environment of sustained coldness and criticism is more likely to do so, and may be the setting for significant harm. It is suggested that to focus scarce resources and skills solely on investigating specific incidents is not likely to be as cost-effective as assessing the child's and family's wider needs more systematically, and offering a range of support services. The same applies **after** investigation; very few children or parents received any follow up or support, and in up to a third of cases there was another incidence of harm. The research provides revealing statistics, for instance that, of about 160,000 children referred into the child protection process annually, about 130,000 "fall out", usually with little other support being offered.

The research has been criticised for undermining child protection expertise, but in fact it indicates that the process works well in the most serious cases, including sexual abuse, and even in terms of partnership with parents. The research is rather less helpful in indicating what is a "less serious" case which would not merit the full S.47 approach, since practitioners do not have the benefit of research hindsight to identify "one off" abusive incidents. Indeed in some of the well-publicised child deaths of recent years an apparently minor incident has some time later been followed by a fatal assault. What is clear is that pursuing the detail of harmful incidents can take the place of joint assessment and planning for protection and support, which on average receives only nine minutes of case conference time. In fact the "protection versus family support" debate is often a distraction from the real tasks, ensuring that investigations are sensitive and not doubly harmful to the child and that all family support services are aware of child protection and how to deal with concerns effectively and with care.

A detailed study of the effectiveness of a voluntary home visiting service, Home-Start, has been published (Frost *et al.* 1996). Home-Start is a "voluntary organisation in which volunteers offer regular support, friendship and practical help to young families under stress in their own homes, helping to prevent family crisis and breakdown". The study used a number of methodologies including survey data on 305 families and 337 interviews concerning 46 families. Increased interest in outcomes led the researchers to seek evidence of the scheme's effectiveness. They ruled out the use of a control group for the reason outlined on page 29, and statistical indicators such as a reduction in child protection registrations could not necessarily be attributed to a single cause. However, using groups made up of various partners in the work, such as parents, volunteers, and health visitors, they generated desired "outcomes". See also *"Priority Focus"* p74 for the use of consumer groups to generate ideas. According to mothers, volunteers, and professionals such as health visitors and social workers, Home-Start has a powerful role to play in providing accessible and non-stigmatising support to isolated and/or troubled parents before or during a period of crisis. The majority of women saw an improvement in their emotional well-being during the six month study, and also thought that their informal network of support had been extended. A substantial minority also reported improvements in their relationships with either partners (or ex-partners) or professional workers, or both.

CHANGES IN EMOTIONAL WELL-BEING

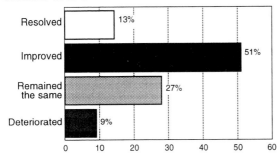

CHANGES IN RELATIONSHIPS WITH PROFESSIONAL WORKERS

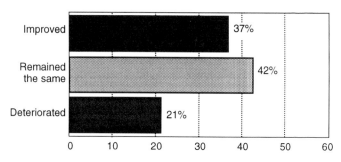

CHANGES IN POOR RELATIONSHIPS WITH PARTNERS/EX-PARTNERS

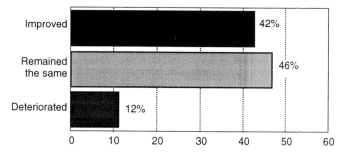

CHANGES IN PARENTING ISSUES

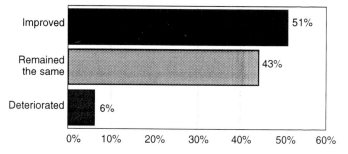

SUMMARY

Very few research studies can "prove" a link between a specific intervention or support provision, and positive outcomes (such as improved IQ) or avoidance of negative outcomes (such as behavioural problems). In the States, one or two large scale, longitudinal studies using control groups have influenced policy on pre-school provision. Evaluations of family support services have also been collated to provide common messages about what works well.

In the UK there has been little research focused on family support itself; government-funded research has largely been concerned with children accommodated by local authorities and with those seen as in need of protection. The latter (HMSO 1995) indicates that although serious child abuse is investigated effectively, too many less serious situations are dealt with solely by investigation without full assessment or any support services, so that the wider needs of the child and family are being missed. Forms of harm and neglect which are just as damaging as, but less apparent than, direct abuse (for instance health problems) may thus be ignored. Recent research into an organised home visiting scheme to support young parents under stress suggests that, in the view of the main partners to the scheme, it has a high degree of effectiveness (Frost *et al.* 1996).

Budgeting and financing

This is the rock on which family support initiatives often founder. Why is this?

1. Of their very nature these initiatives are usually set up by, or with, the "worried well" – or perhaps the "walking wounded" – rather than those with such acute or chronic difficulties that professionals are already heavily involved. As financial pressures increase, so provision is more tightly defined around what is "core", "essential", or "mandatory" and everything else is defined out of funding.

This process is of course a vicious circle in that if it takes a crisis to obtain a service, more events will be defined as crisis, or will have to wait until an actual crisis occurs. High-cost provisions, such as intensive care in hospitals, secure accommodation for serious offenders, and child protection investigations, are always balanced with difficulty against earlier, cheaper, but less-clearly-targeted services such as health promotion, diversionary programmes for teenagers, and support for parents under stress.

Providers of support services tend to go along with these spurious comparisons rather than arguing that a healthy service comprises all three levels of prevention (see chapter on *Relevant theory and research findings*) and that if cuts are to be made they should not fall at one end of the spectrum, thus throwing the system out of balance. They also need to argue that prevention services (as well as treatment or life-and-limb provision) have a firm basis in law (see chapter on *Defining terms*).

2. It is certainly true of social services that some major budgets are dispensed on a case-by-case basis. The "Section 17" budget is often the only identified source of family support funding and, because the law states that money can be dispensed only to particular children in need in exceptional circumstances, this is seen to exclude project or service development funding. This requirement actually only applies to cash payments. The amount and use of S.17 funding vary widely but research by Jane Aldgate and Jane Tunstill has given information on its use and on the priority groups within the wide definition of "children in need".

RISK INDICATORS OF CHILDREN IN NEED

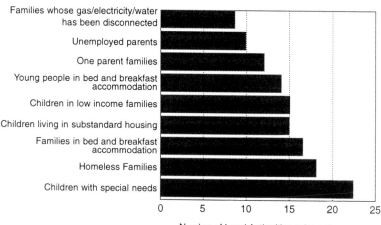

Number of Local Authorities using category

More visionary local authorities have made preventive work a plank of their Children Services Plans across several departments. Each has set aside a proportion of its total budget for this, often totalling an impressive amount and allowing for joint funding with the voluntary sector and/or health trusts. But services are not always monitored adequately, and this puts them at risk.

3. Local small-scale projects face another vicious circle in that the implementors often cannot (or believe they cannot) afford the time and resources to create a project or business plan (see pages 61 and 62). Yet without it they cannot argue for resources. Umbrella and training organisations, such as the National Council for Voluntary Child Care Organisations or the Directory for Social

Change (see Useful Contacts p88), have traditionally provided some of the administrative infrastructure and support to small organisations in the form of policy frameworks, guidelines, research, and training. They too are under financial pressure, but any family support group, however small, needs to find these resources, perhaps by pooling them locally, if it is to survive.

4. Finally, groups are often more involved in the day-to-day activities than in the administration needed to keep those activities going. Administration has almost become synonymous with "waste", yet sound administration is as essential as any other skill in family support work. Essentially, this is about accountability demonstrating to families who use the service and to the wider community that the work is not just for the benefit of the workers but sets out to make a real difference, and being able to show evidence of how resources have been used to that end. Elements of accountability are clear, up-to-date records; independent review; supervision and appraisal; public availability of policies and a complaints procedure; and clear accounts.

The following pages show how financial management and budgeting fit into the planning process, and why they are so vital. A small organisation may be able to do without some of this financial data – but it may never be able to grasp fund-raising opportunities and extend its activities, because the answers to key questions will not be available.

The author is indebted to Pam Craig of Sayer Vincent Chartered Accountants for the notes and exercise which follow.

HOW BUDGETING FITS IN

OBJECTS/MISSION	The aim of the organisation and reason for existence.
TARGETS	Goals which it sets for itself in the medium term (about five years).
STRATEGY	The plan for how the organisation will achieve these targets.
PLAN	Details of the staffing requirements and resources necessary to achieve the plan.
REVENUE BUDGET	The projected revenue income needed and running costs according to the plan – prepared in detail for the year ahead and in outline for subsequent years.
CAPITAL BUDGET	The projected capital expenditure as a list of equipment needed and its cost.
CASHFLOW FORECAST	Based on the revenue and capital budgets, the cashflow forecast will draw the two together. It will take into account the timing of receipts and payments and will show the forecast cash resources and their utilisation if the plan is carried out.
MANAGEMENT REPORTS	Throughout the period of the plan, each budget and the cashflow must be monitored. Actual performance must be compared with predictions.
REVISIONS	The management reports should contain sufficient information to enable conclusions to be drawn from the evidence and decisions to be taken on changes necessary. These should then be incorporated into the plan, budgets, and cashflow forecasts.
ACTION	Because there is an overall plan, management can give staff a clear brief on their tasks and the plan can be put into action!
APPRAISAL	The plan should specify timescales for appraisal and assessment. It should also set out what its performance indicators are. It will then be feasible to assess successes and failures and learn from them.
SUCCESS	Well done! You have passed 'GO' and deserve recognition for your successes!

THE BUDGET PROCESS

Agree Long Term Objectives
Set Short Term Desirable Target
Identify Limiting Factors
Establish Level of Activity
Identify Budget Headings

         – Fixed Costs

         – Variable Costs

         – Mixed Costs

Complete Fixed Cost Estimates
Complete Variable Cost Estimates
Document Assumptions Underlying Estimates
Identifying Sources of Income

         – Certain

         – Probable

         – Possible

         – Variable

Complete Estimates of Income
Appraise Budget – Is it Realistic?
Identify Possible Problems
Prepare Alternative Budgets
Present to Management Committee
Incorporate Amendments
Obtain Approval of Management Committee
Report Against Approved Budget Throughout Year

BUDGETING

1. THE PURPOSE OF A BUDGET

A budget is the conversion of the plans of an organisation into a financial statement. It is important that this process goes on as part of the planning activity as the financial implications of a plan are crucial to its success or failure. In addition, everyone in the organisation needs to be aware of the budget. Although one person may be responsible for its preparation, the budget should be explained at a meeting and adopted formally. The meeting should further ensure that it receives regular financial feedback so that variations from the budget are known and can be dealt with. Every organisation should have a budget prepared well before the beginning of its financial year, so that there is time for discussion and amendment.

2. WHERE TO START

A budget is prepared on the basis of a given level of activity. All this term means is the amount of work the organisation is aiming to achieve in a given time. When planning the year ahead, the main constraining factor on your organisation should emerge. This may be the number of staff, the amount of income, the demand for product or services, or the size of your premises. Obviously it will depend on your type of work as to what your particular constraining factor is. It is also possible to think of ways of changing the constraint. For example, you may decide to recruit more staff, obtain more income, run an advertising campaign to increase the demand for your product or services, or move to new premises. Any of these decisions would mean that a very different plan would be devised. In practice, therefore, you should start by working out a budget based on your current level of activity, and then the effect of changes such as moving premises, recruiting more staff, etc. can be incorporated. This means that you can start by looking at the past.

3. PREPARATION OF A BUDGET

Decide what the constraining factor of your organisation was over the past year. Use the following questions to help:

Did we have more requests for our product or services than we could satisfy?

Did our volunteers and staff have too little to do?

Are we on a fixed income?

How much effective time did we have available? (as opposed to time spent on internal administration, meetings, planning work, etc.).

Did we charge enough for our work or product, or too much?

Next, examine your past costs and decide which of these were fixed and which were variable. Fixed costs are those which you would have to pay anyway regardless of how much work you had been doing. In reality, you should interpret this term to mean fixed in the short term, because obviously you could decide on major changes to policy which would affect those costs.

Example of fixed costs are:

Rent and rates;
Insurance on premises;
Building maintenance;
Light and heat;
Office running costs – stationery etc.;
Basic salaries of workers.

Other costs of your organisation may be variable according to the amount of work you are doing or deliberate policy. For example, you may decide to advertise more. These are the costs where you have to make an assumption about the estimated cost based on policy and the information available.

Costs can also be divided into direct costs and overhead costs. Direct costs are those involved in providing the service or producing the goods. Overhead costs are those involved in the premises and running the organisation, including the office administration. These do not equate exactly to variable and fixed costs. However, many overheads will be fixed costs, and many direct costs will be variable.

These are basic definitions, but in practice you have to use your own judgement. Taking all the known factors into consideration, you may come up with different answers to the textbook case, and if you have used your understanding of the principles underlying costs analysis and your knowledge of your own organisation, you have probably got it right.

CASHFLOW FORECASTS

	Month 1	Month 2	Month 3	Month 4	Month 5	Month 6	Month 7	Month 8	Month 9	Month 10	Month 11	Month 12	Total
RECEIPTS													
Grants													
Donations													
Bank Interest													
Conferences													
Publications													
Miscellaneous													
TOTAL RECEIPTS													
PAYMENTS													
Net Salaries													
Inland Revenue													
Publications Costs													
Rent and Rates													
Light and Heat													
Insurance													
Equipment													
Maintenance													
Repairs & Renewals													
Cleaning & Sundry													
Telephone													
Photocopying													
Stationery													
Postage & Delivery													
Reference Materials													
Training													
Travel													
Legal and Professional													
Audit and Accountancy													
Bank Charges													
Capital Expenditure													
TOTAL PAYMENTS													
MONTHLY CASHFLOW													
BALANCE B/F													
BALANCE C/F													

FORMAT FOR BUDGET WITH OVERHEAD ALLOCATION

	Project A	Project B	Project C	Central Admin.	Total
INCOME	£	£	£	£	£
Fees/Sales/Rent	5,000		50,000		55,000
Specific Grants	20,000				20,000
Earmarked Grants		45,000	105,000		150,000
	25,000	45,000	155,000		225,000
EXPENDITURE					
Director's Salary				20,000	20,000
Project Workers' Salaries	14,359	28,717	77,436		120,5122
Administrative Staff				18,000	18,000
Project Direct Cost			40,000		40,000
Publicity		1,000		500	1,500
Recruitment			1,000	1,000	2,000
Office Rent and Services				10,000	10,000
Telephone				3,000	3,000
Printing and Stationery				3,500	3,500
Audit and Accountancy				2,500	2,500
Legal and Professional				500	500
	14,359	29,717	118,436	59,000	221,512
Excess of Income over Exp.	10,642	10,641	10,641	(59,000)	
Central Admin. Allocated	7,375	14,750	36,875		
Total Expenditure	21,734	44,467	155,311		221,512
SURPLUS OF INCOME OVER EXPENDITURE	3,266	533	(311)		3,488

MANAGEMENT ACCOUNTS

PURPOSE

> 1. Provide information.
> 2. Alert staff and management committees to problems (or windfalls).
> 3. Prompt decision-making and action.
> 4. Keep staff and management committees in touch with what is actually happening.

WHAT INFORMATION: COMPARISON OF ACTUAL TO BUDGET

1. Income shortfall/excess;
2. Expenditure above or below target (a comparison is needed);
3. Reasons for variances, e.g. changes in prices, levels of activity, or flaws in original budget;
4. Cumulative position compared with year's budget may be useful when broken down into areas of responsibility, e.g. to inform a project that they can spend so much for rest of year;
5. Cash position.

WHEN AND HOW

1. Present soon after preparation – management reports need to contain up-to-date information;
2. Short and to the point. Understandable. Too much detail can be as bad as too little;
3. Some written or oral report to highlight important areas;
4. Regular;
5. Reliable – information should be reasonably accurate.

DESIGNING AN ACCOUNTANCY SYSTEM

Management accounts and the format of information required for management reports will be a good starting point for designing an accounting system.

A good accounting system should:

1. Provide information necessary for the good management of the organisation;
2. Incorporate controls to ensure that the information is complete and accurate.

MANAGEMENT ACCOUNTS EXERCISE

You are the new treasurer for Greenham Women's Centre. You have been requested by the Management Committee to assist in improving the financial reporting to the Management Committee.

At present, the part-time book-keeper sends a report every now and then to the Management Committee, such as the one attached. She does not personally attend Management Committee meetings.

You are going to devise a new format for financial reports, which can be used regularly. You have an hour to prepare an example report to show the suggested format to the rest of the Management Committee. You will have an opportunity at the next Committee to give a short presentation explaining what the new financial report format will achieve. You will have access to an overhead projector for that presentation.

GREENHAM WOMEN'S CENTRE

FINANCIAL REPORT FOR SIX MONTHS TO 30 SEPTEMBER 1995

	Budget For Year (£)	Budget 6 Months (£)
INCOME		
Grant	38,035	19,000
Membership	400	105
Workshop Fees	5,000	1,400
Social Events – Gross Income	5,000	–
TOTAL INCOME	**48,435**	**20,505**
EXPENDITURE		
Salaries and NI	33,135	14,727
Rent and Rates	5,000	3,030
Light and Heat	700	300
Insurance	300	183
Repairs and Renewals	500	562
Telephone	750	458
Stationery and Postage	750	286
Promotion and Advertising	500	205
Library and Subscriptions	400	185
Childcare Expenses	900	483
Social Events Costs	4,000	–
Workshop Trainers' Fees	1,000	595
Audit Fee	500	–
TOTAL EXPENDITURE	**48,435**	**21,017**
SURPLUS/(DEFICIT)	**–**	**(512)**

INTERNAL CONTROL – SEGREGATION OF DUTIES CHART

	Main Bank Account	Petty Cash	Childcare Cash
CUSTODY	Looking after the cheque	Keeping petty cash tin and paying out on production of vouchers receipts.	Keeping childcare cash and making payments.
AUTHORISATION	Signing the cheque (also initialling the invoice/expense claim to show approved).	Signing the petty cash voucher to indicate authorisation.	Signing the voucher or receipt to indicate float reimbursement is authorised when cheque signed.
RECORDING	Entering cheque payments into cash book, reconciling bank.	Entering petty cash vouchers into petty cash book, and cash drawn from bank.	Entering payments into childcare book.

AN AUDIT OR NOT? THE POSITION SUMMARISED

Income (£)	Non-charitable companies	Charitable companies	Unincorporated charities	Industrial and provident societies
0 – 10,000	No need for audit or compilation report. Accounts must be on 'accruals' basis.	No need for compilation report. Accounts must be on 'accruals' basis.	No need for independent examination or audit.	Full 'accruals' accounts and full audit irrespective of size.
10,000 – 90,000			Independent examination required. May produce 'receipts and payments' account.	
90,000 – 100,000	Compilation report required.	Compilation report required.		
100,000 – 240,000			Independent examination plus full 'accruals' accounts required.	
240,000 – 340,000		Audit by Registered Auditor required.	Audit required.	
340,000+	Audit by Registered Auditor required.			

Note: these will be the **minimum** requirements.

ASSESSING YOUR INTERNAL CONTROL

Budget	Yes/No	Action
1. Is a budget prepared?		
2. If yes, is it approved by the Management Committee?		
3. Are amendments approved by the Management Committee?		
Cashflow		
4. Is a cashflow prepared?		
5. If yes, is it approved by the Management Committee?		
Financial Management		
6. Does the Management Committee receive regular reports comparing actual income and expenditure with the budget?		
7. How frequent are these reports? Annual? Quarterly? Monthly?		
8. Do the reports take into account creditors and debtors?		
9. Do the reports highlight the most important financial aspects of the organisation?		
10. Are the reports discussed by the Management Committee and decisions made?		
Book-keeping Systems		
11. Is the Management Committee aware of the system used?		
12. Does the treasurer review the book-keeping system?		
13. Does the treasurer review bank reconciliations regularly?		
14. Is all cash received banked promptly and intact?		

Authorisation of Expenditure	Yes/No	Action
15. Does the Management Committee have ways of checking that expenditure is properly authorised?		
16. Are there clear procedures as to who can authorise expenditure?		
17. Are the cheque signatories all people who can authorise expenditure?		
18. Are all payments except small sundry expenses made by cheque?		
19. Are payments made only when the signatories are satisfied that the supporting vouchers are valid?		
20. Are all paid invoices marked "paid" and a note of the cheque number and date of payment made on the invoice which is filed in chronological order?		
21. Is petty cash operated on the imprest system?		
22. Does the cheque signatory initial the petty cash book at the time of signing the cheque reimbursing the petty cash float?		
Salaries		
23. Do all alterations to salary rates have to be agreed and minuted by the Management Committee?		
24. Does the Management Committee approve overtime and time off in lieu?		
25. Does the Management Committee approve any payments to consultants or casual workers?		

Summary

This chapter provides an introduction to the process of costing, budgeting and accounting, and the associated authority and controls needed. They are given a separate section because many family support initiatives have foundered because of poor financial information and planning.

Clearly, if a grant is not forthcoming good accounts cannot help, but they will certainly increase your chances. It is also important that the service providers and users – managers, advisers, volunteers, parents – all have an appropriate understanding of the finances rather than these becoming too separate or specialised: everyone needs to know the cost and the value of the service, and to contribute ideas for improvement.

Planning for results

American research suggests that family support programmes tend to focus on a single outcome as a measure of success – for instance, improved cognitive skills in the child – rather than taking into account other dimensions such as improved parent:child interaction or greater use of community networks.

Weill and Jacobs (1988) suggest that at least three dimensions – **the child**, the **parent:child relationship**, and the **parent within her or his family and community network** – should be included in outcome measures. We have seen that more recent UK studies such as that by Frost et al (p33) attempt to identify and and measure a range of desired outcomes. Marsh and Cramer (1992) also suggest that research and evaluation studies do not link the **content** and **intensity** of programmes clearly enough to outcomes – i.e., few studies consider the possible effects of doing more of x activity, or combining x and y activities.

Assessment and planning tools currently in use in the UK reflect our emphasis on individual child development and parental functioning. For instance, the DoH publication *Protecting Children: A Guide for Social Workers Undertaking a Comprehensive Assessment* contains 167 questions of which the majority relate to the child and her/his parents.

Messages from Research and the associated studies do not tell us much about the quality of assessment and planning for particular families, other than that planning was allocated some nine minutes on average of case conference time and that the wider needs of approximately a third of the children conferenced were not dealt with. It seems that even the areas we have focused on, such as health and development, often receive scant attention in our assessments, and consider past events rather than future aims.

PLANNING TOOL NO. 1 – ASSESSING CHILDREN'S NEEDS

A new approach has been introduced in the Looking After Children (LAC) initiative by the Department of Health. Using forms which can be computer-held, social workers are encouraged to set goals or outcomes with children or young people and their families and plan towards them using information on key areas of activity – health, education, work on culture, and ethnicity social functioning, etc. *Messages from Research* adapts these areas of activity to child protection planning: see below.

Planning tool no. 1

A.The wider welfare needs of children being protected
(Note: "Overview" refers to the introduction to Messages from Research)

Farmer and Owen's study showed that the wider needs of 32 per cent of the children who were the subject of a protection conference were not adequately dealt with. This finding is echoed in several other studies, such as those by Cleaver, Sharland, Thoburn and colleagues.

Aim: To compare the child's needs as identified in comprehensive social work assessments with those addressed in protection plans and accompanying services.

Preliminary tasks: Be familiar with pp47-8 in the Overview and summaries of the research by Farmer and Owen, pp61-4 and, if time allows, Cleaver and Freemans, pp59-61; Sharland and colleagues, pp79-81, and Thoburn and colleagues, pp85-7. Select a number of cases which have recently been the subject of a child protection plan. Have the file papers available for inspection.

Option 1: Examine an assessment or review form for each case selected, identify any needs in the following seven areas of the child's life, and draw up a list in a similar form to the diagram.

	Needs
Health	
Education	
Identity	
Family relationships	
Social presentation	
Emotional and behavioural development	
Self-care skills	

Option 2: To do the exercise more comprehensively, the Looking After Children materials published by the Department of Health should be applied. Copies may be available from the local authority social services department or they can be obtained beforehand from HMSO. The materials consist of age appropriate Assessment and Action Records covering seven areas of children's lives listed above. Training materials are also available. (Note : see Planning Tool No. 4 on page 59 for *Key Questions* in planning for children.)

Option 3: Select one or preferably more cases that have been the subject of a child protection conference. Examine the background material made available to the conference and additional material recorded in social work files and assessments. From these, identify the following:
● Child protection needs;
● Other needs which would benefit from services;
● Other needs beyond the reach of services.

Apply the framework above or the Looking After Children schedule appropriate to the child. From these, repeat the previous exercises by identifying the following:
● Child protection needs;
● Other needs which would benefit from services;
● Other needs beyond the reach of services.

Compare the two assessments of need
● Is there any difference?;
● Are these differences important?;
● What needs to be done to meet the unmet need identified?

PLANNING TOOL NO. 2 – IN NEED ASSESSMENTS

As part of the attempt to respond more adequately to children in need and support to their families, some agencies are introducing family support conferences, or children in need assessment meetings. This allows another route for sharing information and planning where the well-being of the whole family, rather than significant harm, is the issue; for instance, when a parent has serious physical or mental illness or there are overwhelming practical difficulties. Such situations may benefit from adapting the Working Together model of case conferences. This has the benefit of status and some familiarity, so that professionals are already aware of the format.

Family support/needs assessment conferences have succeeded in bringing in key professionals such as GPs and head teachers who have expressed concerns about a child or family which fall short of child protection referral.

---

1. An agency with which the family is familiar calls the conference/meeting with the family's consent, identifying key individuals.
2. The parent(s) are involved and present throughout, or if parents are in conflict each attends agreed parts of the meeting.
3. The child's/children's views are sought and represented, and/or they are present if they wish.
4. Each involved agency presents a report which has been discussed with the family, assessing difficulties and strengths, desired changes, and possible ways of achieving them, including resources. The family members present their views.
5. The conference/meeting is chaired with a view to allowing maximum participation and sharing of information.
6. An initial work plan is outlined and a core group appointed which includes the parent(s) to carry it out.
   Recommendations as to resources are made to the appropriate budget holder(s).
7. The groups and the full conference reconvene as necessary.

Some local authorities have revised their data collection around a structured needs assessment in stages; there are sections for the child's development, the parents' or carers' needs, the family's environment, history and culture; adding on specific information about child protection, and/or disability etc. as necessary. Each section can include the parents' as well as the professionals' views. See also Family Group Conferences p76.

PLANNING TOOL NO. 3 – GROUPING ASSESSED NEEDS

Another approach has been used by researchers at Dartington to devise an easy-to-use planning tool which allows a team or agency to take a random sample of needs being presented in up to a hundred cases, allocate them to 'needs groups', and come to a view as to whether the services currently on offer in a particular area meet these needs. Aggregated assessments of need are an important requirement for planning family support, but should be approached with care – needs change over time, so reviews are needed and more than one methodology should be used.

NEEDS GROUPS

A. PARENTING

The child lives with, or has recently lived with, a parent or parents. That is the locus of the need.

A1   PARENTING SKILLS NEEDED

The need is for parent(s) to receive support and help to develop skills in relation to a particular issue, type of behaviour, or stage of the child's development. Other problems may be present but are likely to be eased if this one is addressed.

A2   PARENTING – IMPROVE POOR CARE

The need is for the child to receive much better care and protection at home than now. Parent(s) need support and help on a wide range of issues and problems: the child's safety needs monitoring; additional care may be needed; and in some cases children may need to live elsewhere.

There are severe problems across many areas of the family and child's life. There are unlikely to be significant improvements in the near future, or at all. Considerable support will be needed. Children who are scapegoated form a distinct sub-group.

A3   PARENTS' TEMPORARY HEALTH PROBLEM

The need is to supplement parental care on a temporary basis. The health problem is temporary, and usually physical, but the group includes children of mothers with post-natal depression.

A4   PARENTS' CHRONIC HEALTH PROBLEM

The child needs care, and sometimes protection and monitoring. Some supplementary care is needed and attention/help/support is needed to address the parents' health problem(s).

Other problems are present, but the difficulties facing the child are likely to be reduced if health is addressed. The group includes children of parents with long term physical or mental health problems and those affected by alcohol and substance misuse.

A5   PARENTS' NEED PRACTICAL SUPPORT

The need is for parents to receive specific practical support in relation to a specific problem. It includes the need for information, advice, and practical help in relation to children with disabilities and the need for help with problems over finance and housing.

A6   EFFECTS OF TRAUMA ON PARENTS

The need is for the parent or carer to live or cope with or understand a traumatic event or events in order to stop if interfering with other aspects of their life and ability to parent.

There is a similar group for children.

B.   FAMILY RELATIONSHIPS

In this group, difficulties between the adults, or between adults and other family members, adversely affect the relationships in the family – and hence the parenting, this often affecting the child's behavioural development both inside and outside the home.

B1   PARENTS' NEED TO UNDERSTAND THE EFFECT OF THEIR BEHAVIOUR ON THE CHILD AND CHANGE THE BEHAVIOUR

The need is for parents to get some understanding of how the problems in their relationship are affecting the child, and to change the behaviour. The basic needs of the children are being met but it is not a nice environment in which to live.

The children are not particularly difficult themselves but tend to be causing some concern, usually because of minor emotional or behavioural problems. If nothing is done, some will move into the next group (B2). It includes a sub-group of children who are used as pawns in the conflict between separated parents.

B2 ADULT UNDERSTANDING AND A CHANGE IN BEHAVIOUR ARE NEEDED, PLUS THE CHILD'S PROBLEM BEING ADDRESSED

The need is for the adults to understand the effects of their relationship difficulties and to be given help in overcoming them to enable a change in their behaviour. In addition, the children need help in understanding why the adults behave as they do. The children also need to be given help, support, and, in some cases, control where their behaviour is anti-social and/or self-harming.

The children are unhappy and their behaviour problems severe – these include violence, drug-taking, self-harm, or eating disorders. They tend to be anti-social rather than delinquent. Schools are struggling to keep hold of them.

B3 PROBLEMS AROUND ADULT:CHILD RELATIONSHIPS, INCLUDING CONTACT AND IDENTITY ISSUES

The child has a need for a continuing relationship with an absent family member or members. There is no immediate expectation that an absent parent will parent. There is a need for contact to be established, monitored, and continued.

Problems of loss and identity cause the children to misbehave – leading to concern and irritation, and sometimes exclusion from school.

C. CHILD'S SITUATION

c1 CHILD'S BEHAVIOUR NEEDS CONTROLLING

The child needs to be controlled, and help is needed to ensure that their behaviour does not cause problems in other areas of life, such as school or family relationships. Parents may need to be involved in addressing the problem and may also need help in relation to parenting and/or relationships.

There are frequently, but not always, parenting problems (as in A) and/or family relationship difficulties (as in B), but either these are not the causes of the child's misbehaviour or unhappiness or the behaviour is so extreme that it is a primary need in its own right.

The group includes children deemed to be beyond parental control. A distinct sub-group is the young abuser.

c2   CHILD'S HEALTH PROBLEM

There is a need for specific and defined (and possibly long term) help, arising from the child's physical or mental health, or from a disability. There is often a very obvious need for co-ordination between health, education, and social services, and for links with adult services as children become adults.

c3   EFFECTS OF TRAUMA ON A CHILD

There is a need for the child to live with, cope with, or understand a traumatic event or events, to stop them interfering with other aspects of the child's life. The trauma can result from a variety of events – sexual abuse, physical abuse, loss of a close relative or friend through suicide or other death, rape or the witnessing of a rape.

There is a similar group for parents.

D.   PROTECTION

The primary and pressing need is to provide immediate protection for the child. Once that has been done the child will move into another need group.

E.   OTHER

There is a need for an enquiry only. There is no other need because of one of the following reasons

- the child is looked after by another local authority;
- the child and family are coping, following abuse by a professional or someone else outside the family;
- the allegation is unfounded;
- there is a referral but there is no need, except possibly for information.

F.   OUTLIERS

A few cases that don't fit with any of the need groups.

The exercise can take anything from a few hours to days, but once a more realistic profile of children in need is available workers can be creative about the kinds of skills and services that will best match that profile. This is important whether youare a purchaser or provider

PLANNING TOOL NO. 4 – FRAMEWORK (PLANNING FOR CHILDREN) DEVELOPED FROM SSI MATERIALS (1991)

1. Is the child at the centre of the planning process in your department?

What is the system for consulting the child about her views on her own situation?

Have you checked that the language you use is accessible; that time-scales are child centred?

Are the child's natural parents genuinely involved in the process?

What is the range of techniques in use for communicating with the child?

Is the child's own account of her situation and preferences listened to, recorded, protected?

2. Has all the information about the child's family and community network been collected?

Has the father been consulted?

What about the wider family – grandparents, aunts, and uncles?

What is the real importance to the child of the community she belongs to?

Are there religious, cultural, or linguistic factors which must be taken into account.

Have you considered whether the child has special needs?

What is the future for the child in the community in which you are considering them for placement?

3. Has the policy context for each individual child been fully explored?

Have you checked on the regulations and guidance which are relevant to this case?

Are you familiar with your department's policy on child care cases?

What research findings are helpful?

Is training available in your department which helps to fill in the policy and research background? Can dissemination be improved?

4. Is there a clearly defined assessment process for major decisions?

Where is it written down? Is it well known or routinely and
regularly used?

How are assessment decisions recorded? Who maintains the
records; who is responsible for updating them?

How frequently are planning decisions reviewed? Is the child
involved in the review?

5. What is the department's system for ensuring that all the relevant partners collaborate in the plan?

Natural parents, foster parents, carers, the wider family, the child
– have they all been considered and involved?

Is there a system for involving all relevant staff: specialist social
workers, legal advisers, residential staff?

What about other departments? Is there a system for providing
advice and collaboration in relation to health or education?

Have special needs been considered? Have specialist equal
opportunities advisers been consulted?

6. Is this how your planning process works in practice?

The plan
action
information
review
The central actor: the child.
The key partners: parents and carers.
The most effective tool: an informed, recorded, reviewed plan.

Check all the elements again: information
                                                  assessment
                                                  decision making

Projects or provider units in the community often struggle
with deciding on outcomes and setting targets, believing

them often to be unrealistic and too closely tied to funding
decisions rather than service needs to be helpful. These
criticisms are understandable but they can also be the
result of an unwillingness by project managers to confer
and plan actively with their staff and users. Unfortunately
if they do not plan for themselves they are likely to have
plans imposed – or worse, be 'planned out' because their
achievements go unrecorded. Some reasons for **not**
planning include

- It seems easier to deal with events on a day-to-day basis rather than plan ahead;
- People deal with comfortable or familiar problems or situations and ignore the tricky, nasty, or boring ones;
- They feel they are at the mercy of external forces...and use this as a reason for doing nothing;
- No one wants to commit themselves to doing anything specific because they can be seen to fail if it is not achieved;
- People do not know how much anything will really cost.

Adirondack 1989

Helpful formats for a project plan or proposal are
provided in the inserts. They simply provide a starting
point and can be adapted as necessary.

It is useful to remember the US research which
indicated that family support programmes tend to focus
on one set of outcomes – usually, in the States, to do with
child development. These outcome, are of course
significant but parent:child relations, or the parents' own
well-being and support networks, may be equally
important in the medium to long term.

- Is it usual to ask whether an intervention has in fact benefited the child or her/his parents and how we might measure the benefit?;
- What outcomes do children and families who use the project want – have they been asked?;
- What do staff and/or referring agencies want? Is there common ground and can the different aims be reconciled? (if not these conflicting expectations must be addressed);

▶

- Once the agreed outcomes are clear, other issues tend to be easier to tackle, i.e. the short term goals or targets, specific activities and costings, and the standards and outcome measures or performance indicators. These can be summarised as – what is expected of us and what do we expect of others?

In the chapter following, we give examples of specific projects which have been planned successfully and, as a result, been able to give evidence of their achievements. Equally, they can show that they are willing and able to learn from mistakes or failed attempts. When failures are closely examined, there are often learning points that make them worth the effort as indicators of how to improve the service. Funding agencies are much more likely to be positive where there is evidence of this kind of learning from mistakes than where managers claim success without anything to back the claim up.

4. Planning Statement/Proposal for Service/Development

- Background (why? including any statement of Mission or Values)
- Aims (can be broad and aspirational)
- Objectives (specific and related to time frame/resources)
- Outcomes (what will be different?)
- Activities (how?)
- Performance Indicators /Measures (criteria, qualitative and quantitative)
- Risk Assessment (what would be disastrous, and how to plan this out; what dificulties could arise eg loss of finance, staffing; contingency plans)
- Research /Evaluation/Monitoring (methodology, including user views and independent observations: what is the review method – how will learning be applied?)
- Resources (management/staff/premises/equipment/funds). Attach previous year's accounts and budget/forward costings for the service
- Human Resources A skills/competencies profile should be drawn up
- Management and staff issues, e.g. accountability, policies, training (include structural map)
- Summary
- List of key contacts: names, positions, and contact numbers – address/telephone/fax/e-mail, etc.

(See also chapter on *Defining terms*).

SUMMARY

This chapter has given several formats which provide a structure for planning family support work, firstly in the shape of an exercise which studies individual child protection cases for their wider family support needs, then an outline for assessment conferences which start to bring people together to address these issues. We also look at planning tools for use on a larger scale, to aggregate scores of cases so that resources can be redirected if necessary.

Having planned to meet the individual family's needs and for those of the wider group, a specific piece of work or project may emerge and a format for a proposal to take such a project forward is provided, which could then be elaborated into a Business Plan.

Activities – practical illustrations

A.   AN ADVISORY SERVICE FOR ASIAN WOMEN IN EAST LONDON

Excerpts from the service's annual reports and other data are set out here. They illustrate first the content of the service, second the quantitative data collected (numbers of people seen, nature of enquiries, some of referral, etc.), third achievements, and fourth options for future development and evaluation, developed with the University of Warwick.

This represents a massive amount of administration on top of direct service provision, but the effort has hitherto ensured the project's broad basis of support and growth at a time of funding cuts.

ASIAN WOMEN'S ADVISORY SERVICE

MENTAL HEALTH AND COUNSELLING

Asian Women's Advisory Service was formed in 1992 by the staff members and the Management Committee of the Asian Women's Support Group. The project was originally set up to meet the demands and the specific needs of women with mental health difficulties. It is a resource rooted in the Asian community, with an acute awareness of community needs, committed to the provision of counselling and support to Asian women. Women seeking help may be isolated through their language and culture; stressed and/or depressed; using tranquillisers; coming from psychiatric hospital; suffering from family breakdown; experiencing domestic violence; housebound; single parents.

The women users of the centre as well as outside voluntary and statutory organisations continued to refer women needing supportive counselling because this project was then and still is the only mental health/counselling project for Asian women in the borough.

On receiving a small grant, the project was able to appoint two part time counsellors for 17½ hours per week in total. As the project became more popular and meeting the needs and demands widely in the borough (as well as the neighbouring boroughs) the funding authorities acknowledged the essential resource and later allocated moneys to support the need to increase the hours.

In 1995 AWAS was able to increase the hours for the current counsellors, who have been with the project since 1992, and also managed to appoint another qualified counsellor/development officer to meet the identified gaps. Since the project grew, with more referrals being received, it became even more necessary to acquire another office, a separate counselling space to respect the confidentiality of the clients, as well as a space for administrative work.

In June 1995 AWAS moved into a small office, also using the women's centre for a weekly self-help group.

Apart from providing therapeutic and supportive counselling, other activities of AWAS include facilitating a weekly self-help group, organising and providing training for women in the community to become counsellors and advocates, training women users of the mental health system to become more aware and assertive in order to have their needs met by the service providers.

CLIENT MONITORING 16 DECEMBER 1996 – 20 DECEMBER 1996

Total No. Clients	Drop In	Tel	Outreach Visits	New	Old	Beng	Guj	Urdu Hindi	Punj
96	57	37	2	10	86	46	16	22	12

There are three main aspects of the programme:

- Motor Vehicle Mechanics and Working Sessions;
- Discussion Groups;
- Motor Sport Activities.

A)   MOTOR VEHICLE MECHANICS AND WORKING SESSIONS

The motor vehicle workshop sessions include the following topics:

1. Introduction to the project, the project's rules, health and safety in the workshop, and expectations;
2. Explanation of tools and their uses;
3. Basic car mechanics, explanation of mechanical aspects of the motor car, and identification of parts;
4. Mechanical safety checks which should be carried out by all drivers of motor cars, i.e. oil, water, brakes, tyres, steering, lights, etc.;
5. Servicing and repairing motor cars;.
6. Preparation of cars for banger and Mini car grass track racing.

B)   DISCUSSION GROUPS

Discussion groups are held at the end of each workshop session and cover the following issues:

1. Legal requirements for driving a motor vehicle;
2. The reasons for legislation regarding motor vehicle;
3. Consequences of motor vehicle offending to both offenders and victims;
4. Clients' views and opinions regarding the programmes;
5. Any other issues that arise during the programme.

C)   MOTOR SPORT ACTIVITIES

The Motorvators project can provide clients with a chance to take part in banger racing, Mini car grass-track-racing events, and motor-cycle trials riding. The project runs a ladder system for clients wishing to take part in these events. In order to qualify for them clients must attend 20 sessions, take part in the discussion groups, and not be arrested for any motor-vehicle related offences.

To date, the project has attended seven Mini grass-track meetings and eight banger racing meetings, enabling 22 clients to take part in these events. In addition to the car racing events the project has run six motor-cycle trials-riding day trips with eight clients taking part. Attending these events has proved very demanding for both staff and clients as they involve an early start on Sunday mornings, considerable travelling time, and a long day at the track keeping the vehicles running. A few clients have found this a bit much and have not attended though they have qualified for driving on the ladder system. However, the majority have found that taking part in motor racing events an exciting enough prospect to justify getting up early on a Sunday morning.

Overall Results

Over the 18 months the project has been operating, 101 referrals have been received, of which 60 resulted in a programme at Motivators. Of these, 22 have completed their programmes in full, 20 part of them, and 10 are still attending. The remaining eight did not attend regularly. Those who were subject to conditions of attendance but did not comply with their order were recommended for breach proceedings.

The majority of referrals have been in respect of repeated offences with many being seen as persistent offenders. Most clients who have attended well have shown a significant reduction in offending while attending their programme. The project has neither the resources nor had a sufficient time period to accurately track clients after completion of their programme. It has therefore been impossible to ascertain offending rates after programme completion.

Conclusion

The project has aimed to reduce 'motor-vehicle-related crime', covering interfering with a motor vehicle to causing death by reckless driving. The motivation behind these offences is also wide ranging. It is clear that Motivators cannot successfully address all crimes that are seen as motor vehicle related. However, the project has worked with over 50 young people convicted of motor–vehicle-related crimes with only a few known to have reoffended. The project has been particularly effective in working with young people who commit crimes in order to experience the thrills and excitement of driving. These youngsters have been given a legitimate chance to express their interest in motor vehicles and hopefully have learnt to take a more responsible attitude towards driving. It has proved more difficult to work with youngsters whose offending is motivated by financial reward. However, it is hoped that these too will have gained a more responsible attitude towards driving.

B2 PREVENTIVE GROUP WORK PROGRAMMES

1. THE PROGRAMME

> The programme contained the following elements:
> 1. Health and safety in the workshop;
> 2. Basic use of tools and equipment;
> 3. Identification of car parts;
> 4. Motor-car maintenance;
> 5. Legal requirements for the use of motor vehicles on the road, and the reasons for them;
> 6. Motor-cycle maintenance;
> 7. Motor-cycle-trials riding trips;
> 8. End of group evaluation questionnaire.

2. RESULTS

To date the project has completed three outreach and three preventive group work programmes. Each programme was attended by eight young people. These programmes consisted of 16 workshop sessions and three day-trip motor-cycle trials-riding sessions. Twenty of the 24 young people who attended completed the programme in full. The four who dropped out gave other commitments, e.g., schoolwork and other youth club activities, as the reason for not continuing. On completion of their programme the young people were asked to fill in an evaluation questionnaire, the results of which were that the young people had enjoyed the programme, which had developed a greater understanding of motor vehicles and helped them take a more responsible attitude towards driving. They also expressed the view that more motor sport activities would make the scheme more enjoyable. The project is not aware of any of the young people who attended this scheme getting into trouble with the police.

First Group: November 1994 to February 1995	
People benefiting from the project	No. of young people
Black	7
White	1
Asian	0
Other	0

Second Group: March to May 1995	
People benefiting from the project	No. of young people
Black	7
White	1
Asian	0
Other	0

Third Group: July to October 1995	
People benefiting from the project	No. of young people
Black	6
White	1
Asian	0
Other	1 (Chinese)

3.   ANALYSIS

Over the 18 months period of this evaluation, the Motorvators Project has provided programmes for 84 young people between the ages of 14 and 25. They have ranged from those seen as being at risk of being in trouble with the police through to those who have committed numerous motor-vehicle-related offences. Both the nature and the motivation behind these offences have been diverse. The project has been particularly successful in working with youngsters who have got into trouble through their passion for motor vehicles. Those who have got into trouble for financial reward have proved more difficult to work with.

However, the majority attending the project have shown a significant reduction in offending. The preventive group work programmes have proved successful, with 20 out of 24 attenders completing their programmes in full. To the project's knowledge, none of these have subsequently been arrested for any motor-vehicle-related crime.

The project has fallen short of its original target figure of 110 places per year. This target has proved unrealistic. At present the project is working flat out to cope with its existing work-load.

With the resources available a target figure of 60 places per year would be achievable. It remains to be seen if such a work-load would be seen as cost effective. The project has a provisional agreement for funding from the Inner London Probation Service and social services, but City Partnership funding ended in March 1996. The loss of this funding left a large budget deficit. The Rainer Foundation has applied for funding for one of the project's worker's posts in order to make up this deficit.

The project has been hampered by lack of administrative support although a half-time administrative post has been budgeted for. It has not been implemented because of lack of office space.

The cost of renting the premises from Rail Track has been a financial burden hampering the progress of the project. At present Motorvators is short of a part-time project worker to carry out the preventive group work programme. In order for the project to have a successful future these problems will have to be resolved.

C. PRIORITY FOCUS

This is a computerised survey tool used successfully with, and by, children and young people to discover their views, for instance about play and leisure facilities, discipline, or crime prevention. The excerpts are from Priority Focus publicity material and outline the method as used with adults. Local authorities and large voluntary organisations have used this approach with young people to assist them in presenting their views, for instance as part of the development of the local authority's Children's Plan. The following is an example of the method in use and is taken from a report by Priority Focus.

There are five stages in a priority search survey:

Stage 1:   Planning

A member of the Priority Search Team works with the client who is commissioning the survey to clarify the issue or problem that they wish to tackle. That issue is then turned into an 'open' question that will generate positive ideas and solutions.

Having decided the question, the planning process identifies other practical arrangements necessary for a successful survey, including

- identifying an accurate sample of the population to be surveyed;
- agreeing on the various ways the population can be broken down (e.g., gender, age, race, etc.);
- identifying the interviewers who will take the questionnaire out to the population to be surveyed;
- considering any training the interviewers will need.

Stage 2:   The Focus Group

The Focus Group of about 20 people, who are a representative cross-section of those to be surveyed, is recruited. This Focus Group session is the point where the ideas or solutions for inclusion into a questionnaire are identified.

We run this session using an approach which respects those present as being the real experts on what is needed to solve the problem in hand. All are encouraged to express their ideas or solutions to the agreed open question. The ideas people generate are written on hexagons which are placed on a magnetic board for all to see. The Focus Group session takes about three hours to complete.

Stage 3:   Production of the Questionnaire

Once the Focus Group is over we take the ideas and, using the Priority Search software package, enter them into a computer.

The format of the questionnaire produced is less familiar than the usual 'tick box' variety. People therefore need to have the questionnaire explained to them and be shown how to fill it in.

Each solution is randomly paired off with another one three times, so the person completing the questionnaire will have three opportunities to show how strongly or otherwise they feel about each solution.

Stage 4:   Completing the Questionnaire

The questionnaire is then taken out to a wider population (up to a maximum of 450) for completion. The person filling it in places a cross to show a preference between the two ideas or solutions in each pairing, which one felt best to answer the question.

When the questionnaires are completed, they are returned for scoring and analysis.

Stage 5:   The Results

We produce for the client a report and full set of survey results which show the consensus order of priority for all the people surveyed, the differences, common themes, and trends of all the groupings and categories.   ▶

> ### ◀ Going into greater detail
> There are a number of ways in which the results can be analysed and similarities and differences identified. The main one is to use a 'data-field' sheet, which enables the results to be analysed in greater detail. Each data-field sheet is unique to that particular survey and by using one it is possible to identify the priorities for each of the sub-groups.
>
> Tables compare the priorities for everybody (the consensus) with the results for different groupings.
>
> The longer the bar, the stronger the sub-group's preference for an idea or solution.
>
> ### Survey Report
> In negotiation with the client, we shall provide an illustrated report of the survey with a commentary on the significance of the results for each of the sub-groups.

The following is an illustration from a Priority Focus report

Focus Groups and informal interviews

Three focus groups were run to ensure the full range of views and opinions of young people were represented. The following groups were ran:

- Mixed young people's group
- Young women's group
- Community group

Individual interviews were also held with young people in different parts of Wybourn.

How the focus groups were ran

Because many of the people taking part were not used to participating in meetings, effort was made to ensure that everyone attending felt relaxed and comfortable. Although the atmosphere was relaxed and friendly, the groups were structured to ensure full participation of everyone and that the issues discussed related to the provision of a resource centre/youth club.

The meetings and interviews were structured around the following open question:

"How can the Wybourn Youth Club/Resource Centre give young people a better life and future?"

Presentation of results

All of the ideas raised in Stage 1 are recorded on the following pages. The ideas have been grouped into themes.

FINDINGS FROM FOCUS GROUPS & INFORMAL DISCUSSIONS GROUPED INTO THEMES

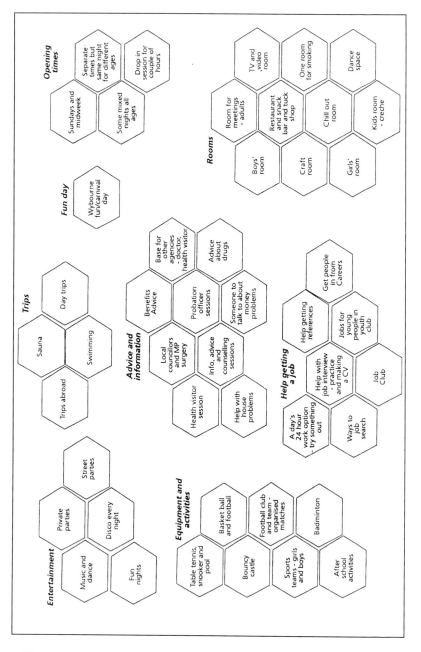

In the first part of the questionnaire respondents were asked to tick all the boxes that applied to them. The results presented are the total numbers giving that reply.

		No. of respondents	% overall
Gender	Male	51	50.0
	Female	51	50.0
Age	12-15 years	32	31.4
	16-19 years	31	30.4
	20-25 years	18	17.6
	26-40 years	15	14.7
	40 plus	6	5.9
How important is it to provide sessions for 8-12 year olds?			
	Very important	36	35.3
	Quite important	47	46.1
	Not important	7	6.9
	Don't know	7	6.9
How important is it to provide sessions for 13-16 year olds?			
	Very important	67	65.7
	Quite important	29	28.4
	Not important	2	2.0
	Don't know	2	2.0
How important is it to provide sessions for 17-25 year olds?			
	Very important	49	48.0
	Quite important	34	33.3
	Not important	14	13.7
	Don't know	1	1.0
How important are sessions for girls only?			
	Very important	26	25.5
	Quite important	33	32.4
	Not important	32	31.4
	Don't know	7	6.9
How important are sessions for boys only?			
	Very important	34	33.3
	Quite important	28	27.5
	Not important	26	25.5
	Don't know	7	6.9
How important is having one room for smoking?			
	Very important	42	41.2
	Quite important	38	37.3
	Not important	21	20.6

THE RESULTS OF THE SECOND PART OF THE QUESTIONNAIRE

In the second part of the questionnaire, respondents were able to rank the ideas in answer to the question:

"How can the Wybourn Youth Club/Resource Centre give young people a better life and future?"

The results of this prioritisation are presented in two ways:

1   Overall priority list – the average results for everyone surveyed is given by listing all the statements in order of priority. This does not mean that the ideas that appear lower down the list are not important. It only reflects the average priority given to an idea when compared with all the other ideas.

2   Bar charts – the differences in priorities between sub-groups can be represented graphically by the use of bar charts. These give the top ten priorities for each sub-group where the length of the bar represents the order of priority ie the longest bar represents the highest priority, the second longest the second highest priority etc. The length does not reflect the actual score given to that statement

Overall priorities for everyone
1   Support for young people in trouble with the law
2   Help with reading, writing and form-filling
3   Help and advice about drugs
4   Trips out
5   Advice on sex, contraception and problems
6   Support for young parents
7   DIY skills, eg carpentry, cookery
8   Help with job applications and interviews
9   Train local people to work in the youth club
10   Have a snack bar/cafe
11   Have a crèche
12   Outdoor sports, eg football, netball, basketball
13   Help to give up smoking
14   Courses to get qualifications eg child care
15   Support and advice on home and relationships problems
16   Table tennis, pool and badminton
17   Have a chill-out room
18   Advice on money problems and benefits
19   Have doctors surgery and health visitor
20   Help to organise local sports team
21   Weights and fitness training   ▶

▶
22	Activities and talks on young young people's issues
23	Have Wybourn street party and carnival
24	Discos and karaoke
25	Music workshops
26	Full-size snooker table
27	Confidence building and assertiveness
28	Aerobics, keep fit and dance classes
29	Have a room just for girls
30	Health and relaxation classes

COMMENTARY

The top three ideas all relate to major social issues affecting young people's daily lives on the estate. They reflect a feeling that help and support is needed with quite serious problems that are affecting the level of welfare on the estate. Most of the ideas in the top half of priority are around being given help and guidance with personal development issues such as giving up smoking. Most of the ideas that are given lower priority are more fun activities such as discos or having facilities such as a full-size snooker table.

COMPARISON BY GENDER

Number in group	102 Everybody	51 All males	51 All females
Support for young people in trouble with the law			
Help with reading, writing and form-filling			
Help and advice about drugs			
Trips out			
Advice on sex, contraception and problems			
Support for young parents			
DIY skills, eg carpentry, cookery			
Help with job applications and interviews			
Train local people to work in the youth club			
Have a snack bar/cafe			
Outdoor sports, eg football, netball, basketball			
Table tennis, pool and badminton			
Weights and fitness training			
Full-size snooker table			
Help to organise local sports team			
Courses to get qualifications eg child care			
Have a crèche			

There is a significant difference in priority between males and females. The males give high priority to support for young people in trouble with the law and help and advice about drugs. Nearly all of the other ideas given high priority are facilities traditionally provided by youth clubs eg football, table tennis. In contrast all of the high priority issues for females are around being given help, support and training to cope with major life issues. Many of the issues in the females' top ten relate to childcare issues and contraception. These don't feature in the males' top ten (advice on sex, contraception and problems is given second highest priority by females but only 14th by males).

D. FAMILY GROUP CONFERENCE

This method of bringing families together to address their own problems rather than have professionals impose solutions is described here by Peter Marsh and Gill Crow of the University of Sheffield.

FAMILY GROUP CONFERENCES, PARTNERSHIPS AND CHILD WELFARE

A research report on four pilot projects in England and Wales.

CONTEXT

Over the past decade there has been considerable interest in the development of approaches to child welfare practice that emphasises the involvement of the user. There are a number of reasons for this development including research that showed that better links were needed between families and children in the care system, and that partnership between users and workers was generally a productive way of working (see, for example, Bullock et al. 1993; Marsh 1993; Millham *et al.* 1986; Thoburn et al. 1995).

The Children Act's principles gave continuing impetus to these developments, and the 1990s have seen the idea of partnership occupying an important place in child welfare policy (Packman 1993).

Despite these pressures, there were continuing practice and policy problems for staff trying to work in a more-partnership-oriented manner (Marsh and Fisher 1992), and the introduction of family group conferences in New Zealand provided an example of partnership in action which seemed worthy of a test in the UK (Marsh and Allen, 1993). With the support of the Family Rights Group a number of pilot projects have been established in the UK; currently, an increasing number of social services departments are planning or running conferences.

What is a family group conference?

Family group conferences are convened by a co-ordinator who has specific responsibilities for this task. The conference is charged with answering two questions:

> *"Is this child (or are these children) in need of care or protection over and above that currently provided?"*
>
> and if so,
>
> *"What would be the best way to provide this care or protection?"*

Professionals give evidence to the conferences, but all evidence must always be shared with the family, and the family has its own closed session during the conferences without professionals present (unless invited by the family). The family will include all members of the extended family significant to the child who are able and willing to come, as well as allowing the possibility of including people willing to act as 'honorary' family, such as godparents or close friends. Children, especially older children, will normally be present at the conference and be free to attend to the process as they wish.

The conferences follow a standard and organised agenda, but the process can be substantially affected by family requests (for example the conference may take place in a family home, or on 'neutral' territory, or it may be in an evening; particular patterns in a particular family may affect the process, for example a grand-parent acting as family 'chair', or an older child welcoming everyone to 'their' conference).

The conference has three stages:

first, full information about the problems is shared by both
    professionals and family;
then, the family debate the issues and produce ideas in a closed,
    private session;
finally, both family and professionals debate the plans generated
    and, if acceptable to all parties, put them into action.

Plans for child protection are developed by the family with professional support, and must be approved by professionals. Under this system family members generally have the greatest role in the development of child protection plans, with professionals providing the family with detailed information and advice, and having the power to alter or veto the plans if they would not protect the child. On occasions where professionals (or family members) cannot agree a plan, court processes will usually be required to resolve the issues.

KEY FINDINGS

● Family group conferences have been used successfully with
  the full range of child welfare problems including requests for
  accommodation, planning for children in the care system,
  physical and sexual child abuse, and neglect.

● The children who have been involved are broadly similar to
  those shown in other studies as facing a substantial risk of
  entry to care, they have covered the full age range, and the
  families have included many where the possibility of wider
  family involvement and their ability to plan safely was initially
  doubted.

● A wide range of family members have been involved in the
  decision making and many have offered resources to help and
  support the child.

  ▶

◀

- Out of the 80 conferences, 74 produced agreements that were fully acceptable to professionals and families and that were agreed by professionals to be in the best interests of the children.

- In comparison with non-family-group conference cases there are indications that children are more likely to have a placement with extended families and that the placement is more likely to be stable.

- The professionals involved think the children are protected by the plans and there are indications of a reduction in reabuse rates.

- Family members are very satisfied with the process, although they find conferences stressful and difficult.

- Almost all the professionals involved expressed support for the model but around one-third of social workers appear reluctant to refer families for a family group conference.

- The pivotal co-ordinator role requires interpersonal, group, and organisational skills to negotiate family attendance and participation at the meeting, a process which can be very time consuming and demanding.

- The costs of services requested by the family were thought to be reasonable and staff thought that the conferences contributed to savings in a number of areas which would cover the direct costs of running them.

- Introducing family group conferences into a selected part of social work practice needs careful planning and preparation over at least a year, plus ongoing training feedback and staff support.

SUMMARY

Examples of very different types and scale of activity are presented in this chapter to indicate the huge variety of aims and methods that could fall under the heading "family support". The first is an advice and counselling service springing from the energy and commitment of women in a particular community whose work meets many of Marsh and Cramer's criteria (1992). It has clear, specific aims and content, it is actively entrepreneurial, seeking out support and resources continually and it is also evidence based, drawing on quantitative and qualitative data.

Secondly, a project using young people's interest in motor vehicles in order to deter or prevent crime, a hard task in an inner city area but one that met with qualified success, because of the realistic approach endorsed by a number of agencies.

Thirdly a survey technique that is simple yet widely applicable and, because young people enjoy computers, has given them direct access to influence planners for perhaps the first time in the UK.

Finally, empowering families (in the widest sense) to take responsibility and share fully in decision making about children through family group conferencing is described by researchers.

Bibliography

A Child In Trust The Report of the Panel of Inquiry into the circumstances surrounding the death of Jasmine Beckford (1985) L.B. Brent/The Kingswood Press

Adirondack, Sandy Merritt (1989) *Just About Managing?* A guide to effective management for voluntary organisations and community groups. London Voluntary Service Council

A Framework for Planning Developed from SSI Materials (1991) Social Services Inspectorate

Assessing Outcomes in Child Care (1991) HMSO

Audit Commission (1994) *Seen But Not Heard* HMSO

Batty, Daphne and Cullen, Deborah (eds.) (1996) *Child Protection The Therapeutic Option* BAAF

Burton, Sheryl (1997) *Where There's a Will There's a Way* NCB

Cannan, Crescy and Warren, Chris (1997) *Social Action with Children and Families* Routledge

Child Protection: Messages from Research (1995) HMSO

Children In Need: Report of an SSI National Inspection of SSD Family Support Services (1996) Department of Health

Fox-Harding, Lorraine (1991) *Respectives In Child Care Policy* Longman

Frost, N, Johnson, L, Stein, M, Wallis L (1996) *Homestart and the Delivery of Family Support* Homestart UK

Gardner, R (1991) *Supporting Families; Preventive Social Work in Practice* National Children's Bureau

Gibbons, Jane (1990) *Family Support and Prevention; Studies in Local Areas* HMSO

Hardiker, P et al (1991) *Policies and Practices in Preventive Childcare* Avebury

Holgate, G (1994) *Intentional Homelessness, Dependent Children and their Statutory Rights of Accommodation* Family Law May

Local Government Association (1997) *Drug using parents: policy guidelines for inter-agency working*

Lynch, Margaret (1992) 'Child Protection – Have We Lost Our Way?' *Adoption and Fostering* 16 No. 4

Marsh, C and Cramer, L (1992) *Organising and Financing Prevention in How to Organise Prevention* de Gruyter

Marsh, P and Crow, G (1997) *Family Group Conferences, Partnership and Child Welfare* University of Sheffield

Munroe-Faure, Lesley and Munroe-Faure, Malcolm (1994) *Implementing Total Quality Management* FT/Pitman

NCH Action for Children (1997) *Factfile*

Newall, P (1991) UN *Convention and Childrens Rights in the UK* National Childrens Bureau

Owen, Hilary and Pritchard, Jacki (1993) *Good Practice in Child Protection* Jessica Kingsley Publishers

Parker, R A (1980) *Caring for Separated Children* Macmillan

Parton, N (ed.) (1997) *Child Protection and Family Support* Routledge

Principles and Practice in Guidance and Legislation (1991) HMSO

Report of a Priority Focus Consultation with Young People Living on the Wybourn Estate (1995) Youth Association South Yorkshire

Report of the Inquiry into Child Abuse in Cleveland 1987 (1988) HMSO

Schweinhart, L J, Barnes, H and Weikart, D P (1993)
Significant Benefits: The High/Scope Perry Pre School Study
Through Age 27 High Scope Press

Smith, Gerrilyn (1995) *The Protector's Handbook* The
Womens Press

The Children Act and Children's Needs (1991) NVCCCO (In
Need Implementation Group)

*The UK's First Report to the UN Committee on the Rights of
the Child* (1994) HMSO

Weill, H B and Jacobs, F H eds. (1988) *Evaluating Family
Programmes* New York

Williams, K and Gardner, R (1996) *Caring for Children*
Longman

Useful contacts and sources of information

National Council for Voluntary Child Care Organisations
Purpose: Advice, support and advocacy for member organisations
Director/Chief Executive/Contact: Erica de'Ath
Address: Pride Court, White Lion Street, London N1
Tel: 0171 833 3319   Fax: 0171 833 8637

Directory of Social Change
Purpose: Information and training for the voluntary sector
Address: 24 Stephenson Way, London NW1
Tel: Publications: 0171 209 5151
Tel: Training: 0171 209 4949   Fax: 0171 209 4130

National Children's Bureau
Purpose: Research, Development, and Social Policy
Director/Chief Executive/Contact: Paul Ennals
Address: 8 Wakley Street, London EC1V 7QE
Tel: 0171 843 6000   Fax: 0171 278 9512

The Parenting Education and Support Forum
Purpose: Promoting parent education and support
Director/Chief Executive/Contact: Hetty Einzig
Address: 8 Wakley Street, London EC1V 7QE
Tel: 0171 843 6000   Fax: 0171 278 9512

Her Majesty's Stationery Office
Purpose: Publication of Government Documents
Address: HMSO Publications Centre, PO Box 276, London SW8 5DT
Tel: 0171 873 9090   Fax: 0171 873 8200
General Enquiries: 0171 873 0011

National Society for the Prevention of Cruelty to Children (NSPCC)

Purpose: As title; projects, Helpline, research, social policy
Director/Chief Executive/Contact: Jim Harding
Address: National Centre (and Library) 42 Curtain Road,
London EC2A 3NH
Tel: 0171 825 2500   Fax: 0171 825 2525

Save the Children UK

Purpose: Social work, advocacy and development
Director/Chief Executive/Contact: Michael Aaronson
Address: Mary Datchelor House, 17 Grove Lane,
London SE5
Tel: 0171 703 5400   Fax: 0171 703 2278

Family Welfare Association

Purpose: Family support and advocacy
Director/Chief Executive/Contact: Helen Dent
Address: 501 Kingsland Road, London E8
Tel: 0171 254 6251   Fax: 0171 249 5443

Homestart

Purpose: Family befriending scheme
Director/Chief Executive/Contact: Brian Waller
Address: 2 Salisbury Road, Leicester LE1 7QR
Tel: 0116 233 9955   Fax: 0116 233 0232

The Children's Society

Purpose: Direct social work, advocacy, and development
Research, information, and social policy
Director/Chief Executive/Contact: Ian Sparks
Address: Edward Rudolf House, Margery Street,
London, WC1X 0TL
Tel: 0171 837 4422   Fax: 0171 837 0211

The Family Support Network
Purpose: Database, Research, and Development
Consultancy
Co-ordinator: Professor June Thoburn
Address: School of Social Work, University of East Anglia,
Norwich NR4 7TJ
Tel: 01603 593557
Co-ordinator: Professor Jane Tunstill
Address: Department of Social Policy and Social Science
Royal Holloway, University of London, Egham,
Surrey TW20 0EX
Tel: 01784 443379

NCH Action for Children
Purpose: Direct social work, advocacy, and development
research, information and social policy work
Director/Chief Executive/Contact: Derek Mead
Address: 85 Highbury Park, London N5 1UD
Tel: 0171 226 2033

Priority Focus
Purpose: Independent Research and Consultancy
Address: Room G9 Town Hall, Surrey Street,
Sheffield S1 2HH
Tel: 0114 273 4024   Fax: 0114 273 4752